Happy Holiday
Quilting™

Edited by
Sandra L. Hatch and Jeanne Stauffer

HOUSE of
WHITE
BIRCHES
PUBLISHERS
SINCE 1947

Editors: Sandra L. Hatch, Jeanne Stauffer
Associate Editor: Barb Sprunger
Copy Editors: Mary Jo Kurten, Cathy Reef

Photography: Tammy Christian, Andree Petty, Nancy Sharp
Photography Assistants: Linda Quinlan, Arlou Wittwer

Production Manager: Vicki Macy
Creative Coordinator: Shaun Venish
Production Artist: Brenda Gallmeyer
Traffic Coordinator: Sandra Beres
Technical Artist: Connie Rand
Production Assistants: Shirley Blalock, Carol Dailey, Cheryl Lynch
Book Design: Dan Kraner

Publishers: Carl H. Muselman, Arthur K. Muselman
Chief Executive Officer: John Robinson
Marketing Director: Scott Moss
Editorial Director: Vivian Rothe
Production Director: George Hague

Printed in the United States of America
First Printing: 1998
Library of Congress Number: 98-70678
ISBN: 1-882138-36-8

Every effort has been made to ensure the accuracy and completeness of the instructions in this book. However, we cannot be responsible for human error, for the results when using materials other than those specified in the instructions or for variations in individual work.

Front cover, clockwise from top left: Quilted Holiday Cards, page 29; Holly Berry Santa Wall Quilt, page 35; Happy Birthday Wall Quilt, page 123; Stained-Glass Cross, page 63; and Sweetheart Roses, page 43. Back cover: Bunnies in a Basket, page 65.

Happy Holidays

*I*f there is any group of people who know how to have a good time, it is quilters. Any time quilters gather together, there is laughter, sharing, and the warm feeling of being with people who care about others and care about what they are doing.

That's what this book is all about. We wanted to give you projects to help you celebrate and enjoy every day of the year. Although the title is Happy Holiday Quilting, we think every day can be a holiday, so we've included wall quilts for special occasions as well as wall quilts that can be used to make any day of the year a day worth remembering. We included birthdays, new births, anniversaries and other special occasions as reasons to celebrate by making an extra-special quilt or quilted project.

We divided the year into seasons as a way of organizing our projects, but many of the quilts we've included may be used for any special occasion. Other projects just need a change of color to fit the occasion or season being celebrated. We even included some lesser-known holidays such as National Pig Day on March 1.

Remember that every day's a holiday with quilting. Pick one of the outstanding projects in this book and begin stitching a quilt that will bring you and others joy and cheer for years to come.

Contents

Spring Fling

Winter Festivities

Autumn Occasions

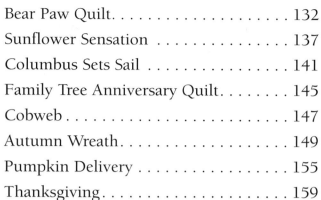

Summer Festivities

General Instructions

Winter Festivities

C elebrate the first snowfall of winter, building snowmen, making gingerbread cookies, the brilliance of poinsettias and times with family and friends at Christmas, Hanukkah and New Year's Day. You'll find wall quilts with beautiful roses for Valentine's Day and a delightfully humorous hedgehog for those who celebrate Groundhog Day. Enjoy festivities all winter long.

Stitch four feathered stars with blue points and white feathers. Set them on-point and add a deep blue background and sawtooth border to complete this quilt. Enjoy the quilt while you are sitting by the fireside enjoying hot chocolate, waiting for the next opportunity to go outdoors and enjoy the activities of winter.
Snowstars Wall Quilt pattern begins on page 8.

Snowstars Wall Quilt

By Jodi G. Warner

Giving the stars a dark blue background with white points conveys the feeling of snowflakes. My cherished winter memories include celebrating the first snowfall and frolicking in the snow as snowflakes soft as feathers gently float down.

Snowstars
11 5/16" x 11 5/16" Block

Specifications

Skill Level: Advanced

Wall Quilt Size: 41" x 41"

Block Size: 11 5/16" x 11 5/16"

Number of Blocks: 4

Materials

1 1/2 yards dark blue print

3/4 yard white print

1 yard light blue print

1 1/2 yards medium blue print

Scraps of various blue prints

Backing 45" x 45"

Batting 45" x 45"

1 spool white quilting thread

Neutral color all-purpose thread

4 3/4 yards self-made or purchased binding

Basic sewing supplies and tools, template material and darning needle or 1/8" hole punch

Instructions

Note: All seams are 1/4" and are included on templates and measurements given for cutting.

Step 1. Prepare templates using pattern pieces given. Transfer grain lines, center lines, positioning dots and any other marks to templates.

Step 2. Using a darning needle or a 1/8" hole punch, make tiny holes at seam intersections on templates.

Step 3. Cut fabric patches (except for E) as directed on pattern pieces.

Step 4. Cut one 18" by fabric width piece each dark blue and white prints; layer with right sides together. Find the true bias on layered pieces (45-degree angle) as shown in Figure 1. Cut ten 2"-wide strips along bias, leaving strips layered as cut.

Step 5. Sew strips right sides together along one long cut edge; press

seam toward dark blue. Place piece E with center guideline on seam as shown in Figure 2. Trace and cut one set of combo squares, leaving sawtooth remnant pieces intact as shown in Figure 3. Seam sawtooth pieces right sides together along straight edge; center and trace E as before to yield a second set of combo squares as shown in Figure 4. Repeat for 128 combo squares.

Step 6. To complete one block, sew four B triangles to A to form block center. Sew E combo units together to prepare eight pairs with triangles slanting right and eight slanting left as shown in Figure 5. Press seams toward dark fabric.

Figure 1
Cut 2"-wide strips along true bias.

Figure 2
Place template E on stitched strip, matching center line on E on seam of stitched strip to make E combo units.

Figure 3
Keep sawtooth edges intact.

Figure 4
Place E on seamed sawtooth pieces as shown.

Figure 5
Join E units as shown.

Unit 1   Unit 2

Figure 6
Piece Units 1 and 2 as shown.

Snowstars Wall Quilt
Placement Diagram
41" x 41"

Figure 10
Complete 1 block as shown.

Step 10. Cut an 11 13/16" x 11 13/16" square medium blue print for J. Sew two pieced blocks to J to make a diagonal center row as shown in Figure 11; press seams toward J.

Step 11. Cut one square medium blue 17 1/2" x 17 1/2". Cut on both diagonals to make K triangles.

Step 12. Sew a pieced block between two K triangles to make corner rows as shown in Figure 11. Press seams toward K.

Step 7. Join D, F and G to E units to complete four sets each of Units 1 to 4 as shown in Figures 6 and 7. Line Units 1 and 2 to short sides of I with point on F matched to hashmark on I leaving bracketed area unstitched as shown in Figure 8. Line Units 3 and 4 to adjacent sides of H as shown in Figure 9; press seams toward H or I.

Step 8. Sew C and CR to E-unit edges which are joined to I, locking

stitching exactly at dot. Stitch C to CR at center seam, locking stitching at dot; press seams toward C pieces.

Step 9. Sew C edges of the I units to top and bottom edges of center square as shown in Figure 10. Sew remaining I units between pairs of H units, holding unstitched I points out of the way, to form side units. Complete seam between I and H units on unstitched edge to complete one block referring to Figure 10. Repeat Steps 6 to 9 for four blocks.

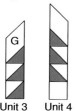

Unit 3   Unit 4
Figure 7
Sew Units 1 and 2 to G as shown to make Units 3 and 4

Figure 8
Sew Units 1 and 2 to I as shown.

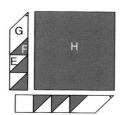

Figure 9
Sew Units 3 and 4 to H as shown.

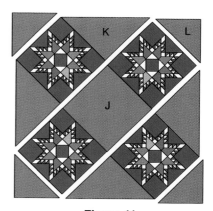

Figure 11
Piece diagonal rows as shown.

Step 13. Cut two squares medium blue print 8 13/16" x 8 13/16". Cut each square in half on one diagonal to make L corner triangles.

Step 14. Sew L corner triangles to center diagonal row; press seams toward L. Join the rows to complete the pieced center.

Step 15. Sew a medium blue M triangle to a light blue M triangle to make 80 triangle/squares. Join 10 squares to make a strip; repeat for eight units—four with light blue triangles slanting left and four slanting right as shown in Figure 12.

Make 4   Make 4

Figure 12
Make pieced border strips as shown.

Step 16. Sew O and OR to N; repeat for four units. Sew an O-N unit between two pieced border strips as shown in Figure 13; repeat for four strips.

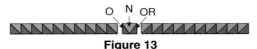

Figure 13
Join a left and right slanting unit with
an O-N unit as shown.

Step 17. Sew a pieced strip to two opposite sides of the pieced center. Sew a P square to each end of the remaining two pieced strips; sew to remaining sides of pieced center. Press seams toward strips.

Step 18. Cut four strips 3 1/2" x 41 1/2" medium blue; sew a strip to each side of the pieced center, mitering corners. Round corners at this time, if desired.

Step 19. Transfer quilting lines to pieced top using patterns given. Trace 1/4" echo quilting lines within C interior star points.

Step 20. Finish quilt as desired referring to General Instructions.

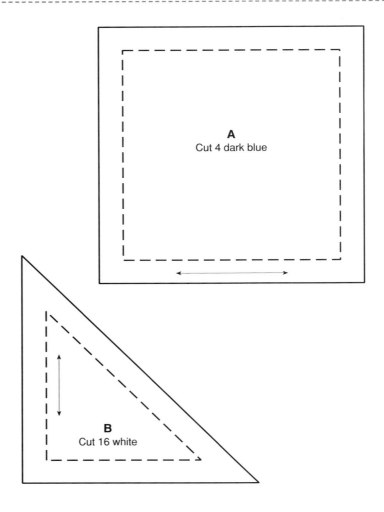

A
Cut 4 dark blue

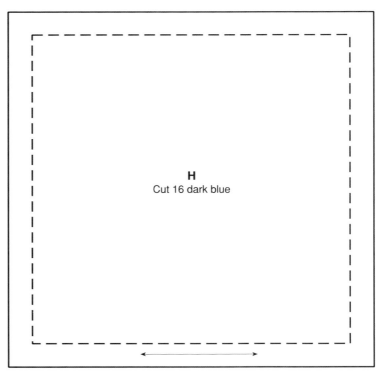

B
Cut 16 white

H
Cut 16 dark blue

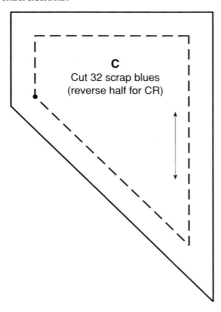

C
Cut 32 scrap blues
(reverse half for CR)

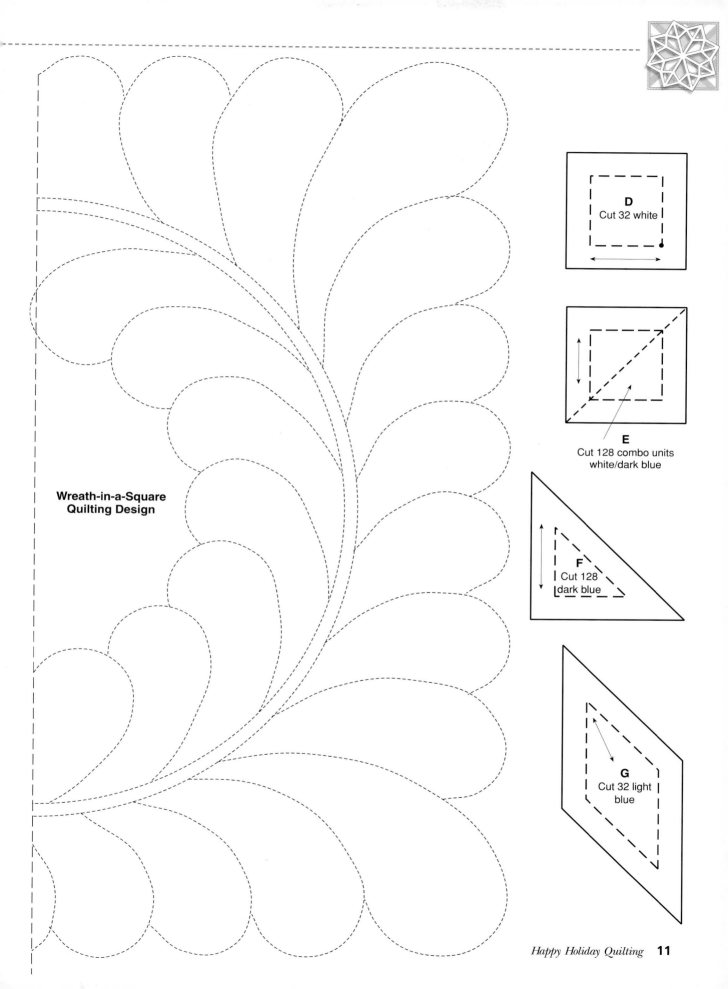

Wreath-in-a-Square Quilting Design

D
Cut 32 white

E
Cut 128 combo units
white/dark blue

F
Cut 128
dark blue

G
Cut 32 light blue

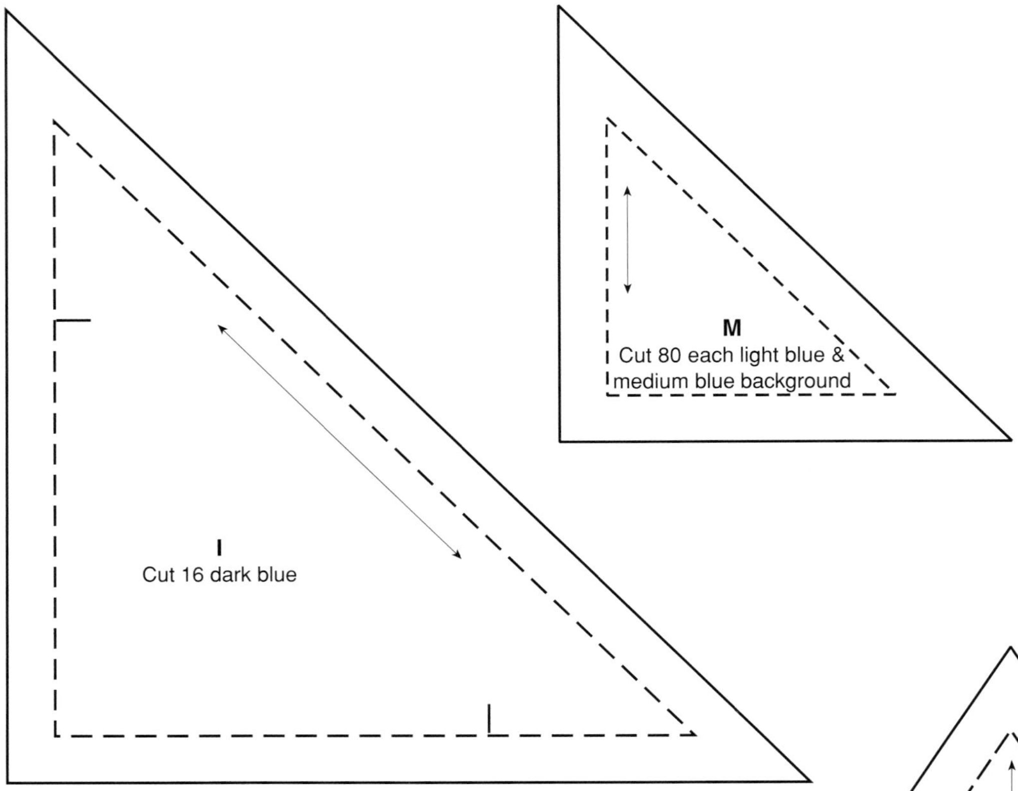

M
Cut 80 each light blue &
medium blue background

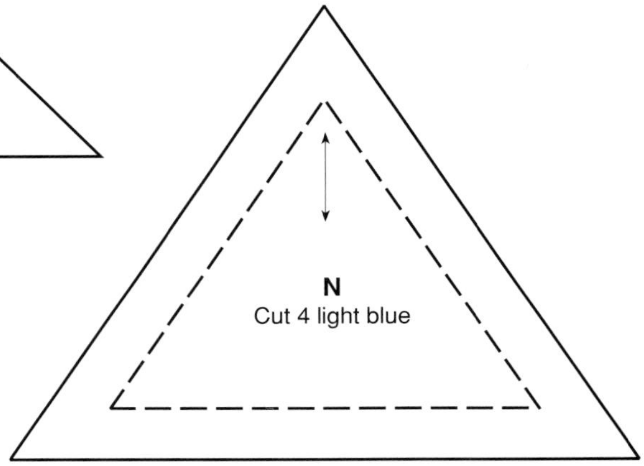

I
Cut 16 dark blue

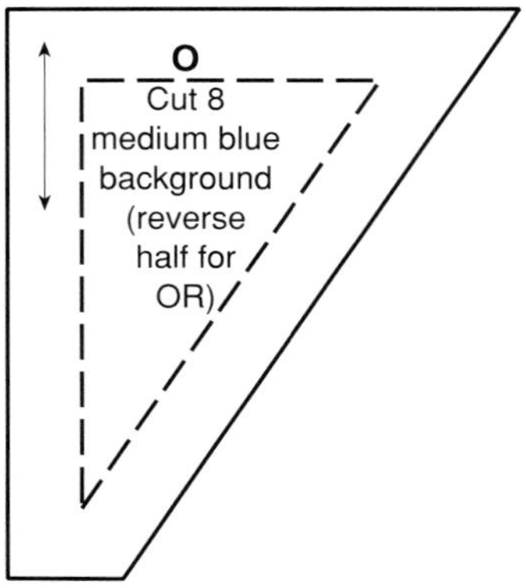

O
Cut 8
medium blue
background
(reverse
half for
OR)

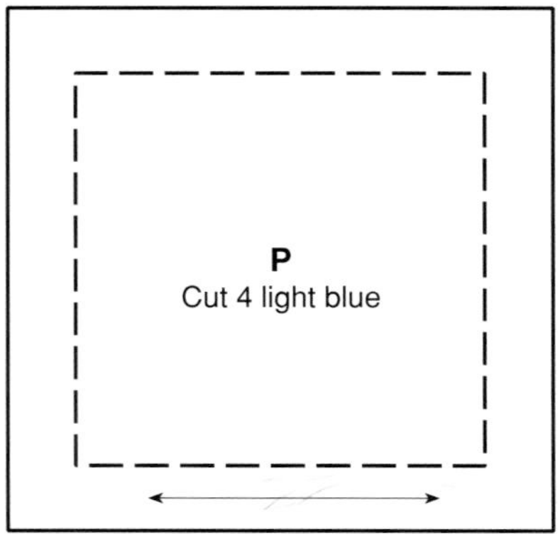

N
Cut 4 light blue

P
Cut 4 light blue

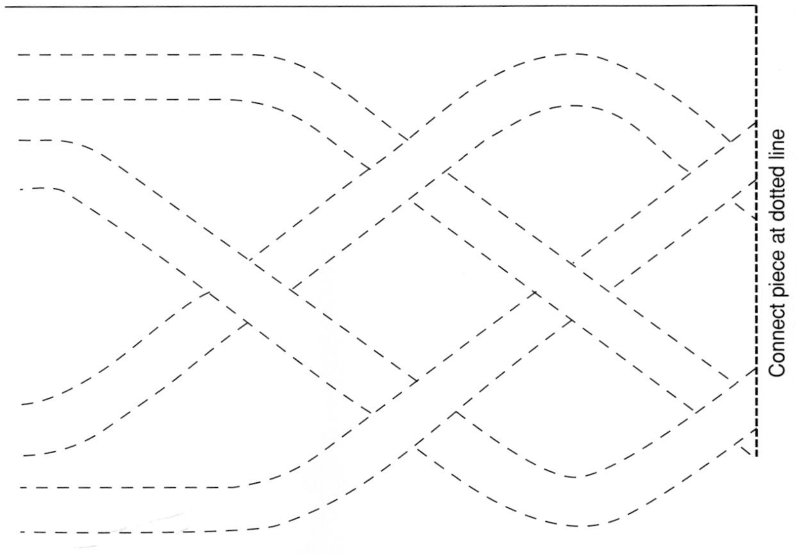

Connect piece at dotted line

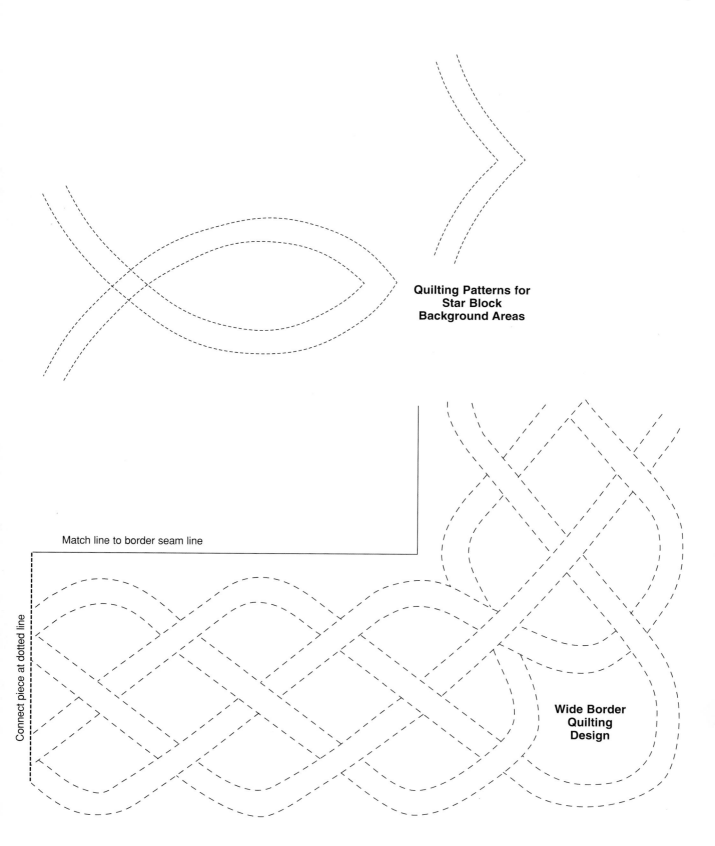

**Quilting Patterns for
Star Block
Background Areas**

Match line to border seam line

Connect piece at dotted line

**Wide Border
Quilting
Design**

Confetti Wall Quilt

By Charlyne Stewart

Just like the new year awaiting us, working on this striking quilt with its random placement of strips and color will be exciting and fulfilling as it comes to life stitch by stitch.

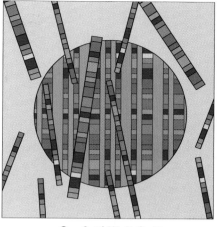

Confetti Wall Quilt
Placement Diagram
40 1/2" x 43 1/2"

Specifications

Skill Level: Intermediate

Wall Quilt Size: 40 1/2" x 43 1/2"

Materials

1 3/4 yards background solid

1/4 yard each of at least 7 solids

1 yard purple solid (commercially dyed from light to dark)

Backing 44" x 47"

Batting 44" x 47"

1 yard pattern paper

1 spool tan all-purpose thread

1 spool purple quilting thread

Neutral color all-purpose thread

5 yards self-made or purchased binding

Basic sewing supplies and tools

Instructions

Step 1. Cut one piece background fabric 41" x 44".

Step 2. Cut an assortment of solids and leftover background fabric into 1 1/2"-wide and 2 1/2"-wide by fabric width strips. Cut three or four strips from each color to create a variety.

Step 3. Stitch the strips together in a random placement. Press seams in one direction. *Note: Strip-pieced section should be at least 32" x 42".*

Step 4. Cut stitched strip into 1 1/2" and 2 1/2" segments as shown in Figure 1.

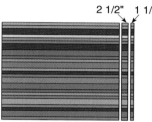

2 1/2"   1 1/2"

Figure 1
Cut pieced section into
1 1/2" and 2 1/2" strips.

Step 5. Cut four strips 1 1/2" by fabric width and eight strips 2 1/2" by fabric width purple solid. Cut into eight 2 1/2" x 32" and four 1 1/2" x 32" segments.

Step 6. Sew purple strips between pieced strips, varying placement of pieced strips.

Step 7. Prepare a paper pattern for a 29" circle referring to Figure 2. Using this pattern, cut a circle from the pieced section as shown in Figure 3.

14 1/2"

Figure 2
Fold paper; make marks at 14 1/2" intervals from one corner. Connect marks; cut on line to make a circle.

Figure 3
Lay circle pattern on pieced section.

Step 8. Fold background piece in fourths; crease to mark center. Fold pieced circle; crease to mark center. Match center of pieced circle on center of background using crease lines as guides for placement.

Step 9. Baste the pieced circle in place. Turn edges under; hand- or machine-appliqué in place on background.

Step 10. Cut away background from behind appliquéd circle to reduce bulk.

Step 11. Arrange leftover strip-pieced segments on background referring to the Placement Diagram and photo of project for positioning suggestions. Turn under seam allowance; baste pieces in place; hand- or machine-appliqué pieces in place.

Step 12. Mark top for quilting varying direction and widths of quilting lines as in circle shape. Hand- or machine-quilt in the ditch of seams and on marked lines as desired.

Step 13. Finish quilt referring to General Instructions.

Snowman Cardigan

By Joy Tennell

The idea for a snowman cardigan came to me while I was looking through old pictures of my husband and sons building a snowman in the backyard. Of course, snowball fights usually interrupted their efforts. Making snowmen and snowballs are fun ways to celebrate winter.

Snowman Cardigan
Placement Diagram
Size Varies

Specifications

Skill Level: Beginner

Cardigan Size: Size varies

Materials

Adult-size blue sweatshirt

1/8 yard blue plaid fabric

1/4 yard green felt

1/2 yard white felt

Scraps brown, orange and gray felt

Scraps green plaid fabric

1/2 yard fusible adhesive

Blue and black all-purpose thread

4 (3/8") black buttons for eyes

6 (1/2") black buttons

2 (3/4") red wooden hearts buttons

6-strand black embroidery floss

1/2 yard white snowflake trim

Fabric glue

2 small safety pins

Basic sewing supplies and tools and fabric glue

Instructions

Step 1. Wash and dry sweatshirt; do not use fabric softener.

Step 2. Fold sweatshirt to find the center front. Mark center line; cut from top to bottom through front layer only.

Step 3. Measure the length of one cut edge. Cut two strips blue plaid 2 1/2" by this length plus 1". Fold each strip in half along length wrong sides together; press. With raw edges even and right sides together, sew a strip down one front edge, leaving 1/2" at top and bottom. Fold the 1/2" ends to backside. Fold the strip to the inside of sweatshirt and baste in place; repeat for second front side. Hand-stitch in place using blue thread.

Step 4. Trace snowman bodies onto paper side of fusible adhesive. Following manufacturer's instructions, fuse onto white felt. Cut out shapes; remove paper backing.

Step 5. Repeat for other shapes as directed on each piece for colors and numbers to cut.

Step 6. Position large snowman on right vest front and small snowman on left vest front; fuse in place.

Repeat for noses, trees, tree trunks and bunny pieces referring to the Placement Diagram and photo of project for positioning.

Step 7. Using 3 strands black embroidery floss, blanket-stitch around each fused shape.

Step 8. Using black thread, sew 3/8" black buttons in place for eyes. Sew three 1/2" buttons down the front of each snowman. Sew a wooden heart in place as indicated on pattern.

Step 9. Tear two strips green plaid into 1"-wide pieces. Tie into bows; attach to snowmen at neck area with safety pins from backside.

Step 10. Cut snowflake trim apart. Arrange individual snowflakes on sweatshirt referring to the Placement Diagram and photo of project for positioning suggestions. Glue in place with fabric glue to finish.

Nose
Cut 1 orange felt

Connect at the dotted line

Connect at the dotted line

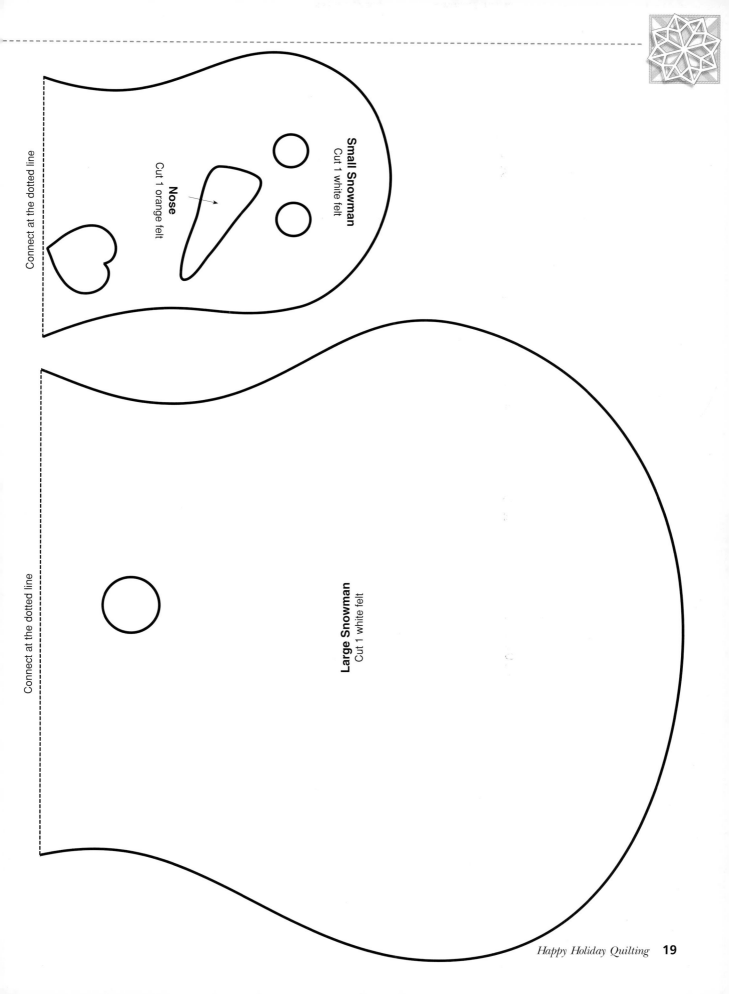

Connect at the dotted line

Small Snowman
Cut 1 white felt

Nose
Cut 1 orange felt

Connect at the dotted line

Large Snowman
Cut 1 white felt

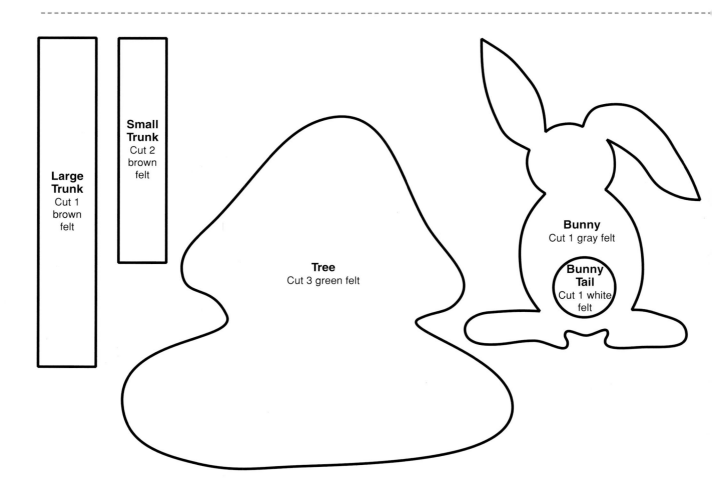

**Large
Trunk**
Cut 1
brown
felt

**Small
Trunk**
Cut 2
brown
felt

Tree
Cut 3 green felt

Bunny
Cut 1 gray felt

**Bunny
Tail**
Cut 1 white
felt

Hedgehog in the Morning

By Norma Storm

This little critter can be made just for fun. His hair is standing on end. It must have happened when he saw his shadow just like the groundhog in February.

Hedgehog in the Morning
Placement Diagram
6 3/4" x 9 3/4"

Specifications

Skill Level: Intermediate

Wall Quilt Size: 6 3/4" x 9 3/4"

Materials

1 fat quarter brown print

1/4 yard light blue solid

Scraps of pale yellow, peach, pale green, light green, 4 shades of blue, lavender, purple, light pink and hot pink solids and green print

1 fat quarter large roses print

Backing 9" x 12"

Batting 9" x 12"

1 spool off-white quilting thread

Neutral color all-purpose thread

All-purpose thread to match rose print and leaf colors

1/4" black button for eye

6-strand black embroidery floss

Basic sewing supplies and tools and tracing paper

Instructions

Step 1. Copy full-size paper-piecing pattern given onto tracing paper. Transfer all numbers and color suggestions.

Step 2. Using paper pattern as a guide and starting with pieces 1 and 2, cut scraps to at least 1/8" larger than spaces for pieces. Lay piece 1 on the space 1 on backside of paper.

Place piece 2 right sides together with piece 1; pin through all layers. From backside, stitch along line between pieces 1 and 2, taking several stitches before beginning and ending of line.

Step 3. Flip piece 2 flat; press. Trim excess from seams before adding piece 3 on top of piece 2. Continue adding pieces in numerical order. Wherever there is a number with an A and B such as 5A and 5B, sew the A piece down first and then the B piece. Hand-appliqué overlapping pieces along seam between the two pieces when necessary. *Note: If you prefer template piecing, use full-size pattern to prepare templates for each piece. Remember the pattern has been reversed for paper piecing.*

Step 4. When piece is complete, trim excess beyond paper background. The finished pieced section should now measure 5 1/2" x 8 1/2".

Step 5. Sew button in place for eye. Using 3 strands black embroidery floss, satin-stitch nose as marked on pattern.

Step 6. Cut two strips light blue solid 2 1/4" x 8 1/2". Sew a strip to the top and bottom of the pieced section; press seams toward strips. Cut two more pieces light blue solid 2 1/4" x 9 1/4". Sew a strip to opposite long sides; press seams toward strips.

Step 7. Isolate two rose shapes from roses print. Cut out each one, adding a seam allowance all around when cutting. Repeat with leaf shapes. Place roses and leaves on lower left corner, overlapping pieced section as indicated on pattern. Appliqué pieces in place using matching thread.

Step 8. Mark border pattern given or one of your own on border strips. Finish referring to General Instructions.

Border Quilting Design

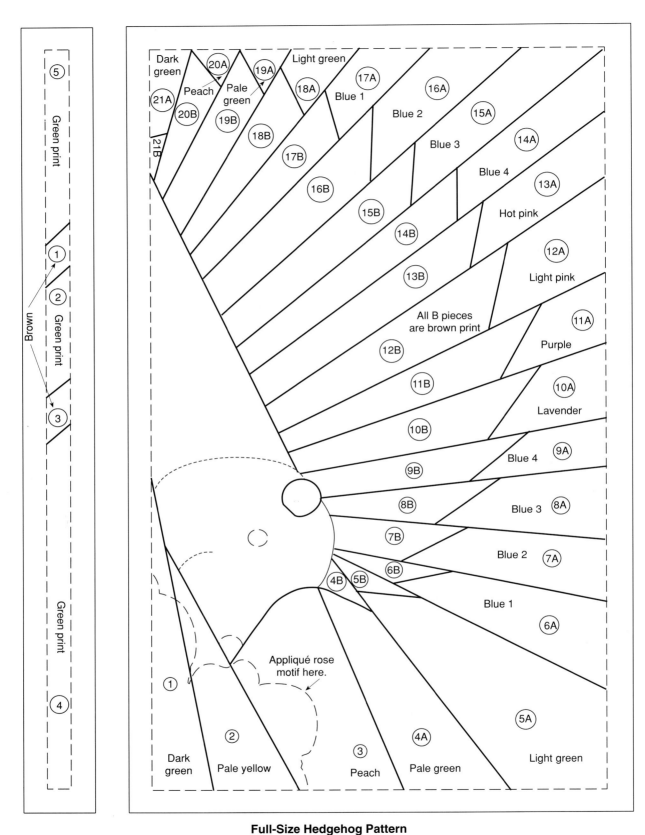

Full-Size Hedgehog Pattern
Pattern is reversed for paper piecing. Seams between A and B pieces of the same number will need to be appliquéd. If template method is preferred, use full-size pattern to prepare templates.

Gingerbread Men Sweatshirt

By Joy Tennell

The inspiration for this gingerbread men sweatshirt came to me when my 11-year-old daughter Amy and I were baking Christmas cookies. At the start of our baking, she requested making gingerbread men. While your cookies bake, whip up this sweatshirt.

Specifications

Skill Level: Beginner

Sweatshirt Size: Size varies

Materials

Adult-size black sweatshirt

20" x 20" square tan felt

Scraps red and green felt

1/2 yard fusible adhesive

Therm O Web Pressing Paper

Black all-purpose thread

6-strand black embroidery floss

4 (1/2") red buttons

4 (1/4") black buttons

Permanent black fabric pen

Basic sewing supplies and tools

Instructions

Step 1. Wash and dry sweatshirt; do not use fabric softener.

Step 2. Trace patterns as directed for gingerbread men, hearts and holly shapes onto paper side of fusible adhesive, leaving 1/2" space around each shape.

Step 3. Cut out each shape, leaving tracing lines. Fuse shapes to felt as directed on pattern pieces following manufacturer's instructions. Cut out on drawn lines; remove paper backing from each piece.

Step 4. Arrange pieces on sweatshirt front referring to the Placement Diagram and photo of project for positioning suggestions. Fuse in place following manufacturer's instructions, using pressing paper to prevent felt from scorching.

Step 5. Using 3 strands black embroidery floss, blanket-stitch around each felt shape.

Step 6. Sew black buttons in place for eyes and red buttons down front of each gingerbread man.

Step 7. Make dots for mouth using 3 strands black embroidery floss and French knots or a permanent black fabric pen to finish.

Gingerbread Men Sweatshirt
Continued on page 28

Gingerbread Men Sweatshirt
Placement Diagram
Size varies

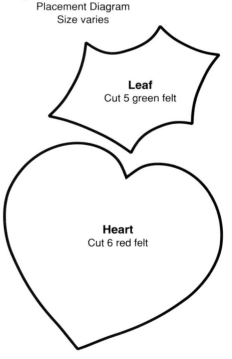

Leaf
Cut 5 green felt

Heart
Cut 6 red felt

Poinsettia Vest

By Joy Tennell

At my house, every Christmas season begins with the purchase of poinsettias. I've had pink and white ones, but red is my favorite because of the deep-colored leaves. They brighten up the house long after Christmas is over. These quilted poinsettias should last for years to come!

Specifications

Skill Level: Beginner

Vest Size: Size varies

Materials

Adult-size ivory-colored felt vest

1/3 yard Christmas green felt

1/3 yard Christmas red felt

3" x 3" square yellow felt

1 yard fusible adhesive

6-strand black embroidery floss

Basic sewing supplies and tools

Instructions

Step 1. Prepare templates for pattern pieces given. Trace six small and eight large leaves on the paper side of the fusible adhesive. Repeat for stems, tracing three small, two medium and one large stem. Trace two of each size petals.

Step 2. Referring to manufacturer's instructions fuse traced adhesive to green felt. Cut out shapes; set aside.

Step 3. On paper side of fusible adhesive, trace six small and six large petals and three small and two large holly berries; fuse to red felt. Cut out shapes; set aside.

Step 4. Trace two flower centers on paper side of fusible adhesive; fuse to yellow felt. Cut out; set aside.

Step 5. Peel paper backing off all pieces. Position small flower, leaf and stem shapes on left side of the vest front, placing two green petals at the bottom. When arranged as desired, cover with cloth and press.

Step 6. Using 3 strands black embroidery floss, blanket-stitch around each shape. Place flower center over petal points; fuse and blanket-stitch in place as before.

Step 7. Position holly leaves and berries on the right front side of vest. Fuse and blanket-stitch in place as before.

Step 8. Center the large flower, stem and leaf shapes on the vest back. Fuse and blanket-stitch in place as before. Add large holly berries and leaves on both sides of flower. Fuse and blanket-stitch in place as before.

Step 9. Blanket-stitch around vest outside edges, armhole and neck using 3 strands black embroidery floss to finish.

Poinsettia Vest Front
Placement Diagram
Size Varies

Poinsettia Vest Back
Placement Diagram
Size Varies

Large Petal
Cut 2 green & 6 red felt

Small Petal
Cut 2 green & 6 red felt

Small Berry
Cut 3 red felt

Large Berry & Flower Center
Cut 2 yellow & 2 red felt

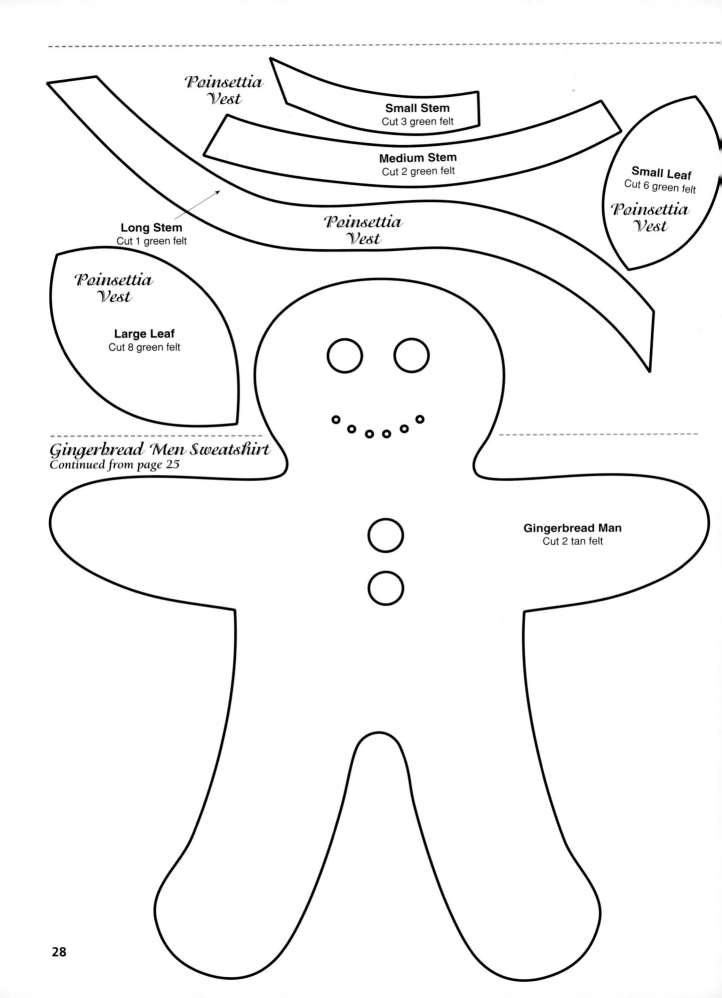

Poinsettia Vest

Small Stem
Cut 3 green felt

Medium Stem
Cut 2 green felt

Small Leaf
Cut 6 green felt

Poinsettia Vest

Long Stem
Cut 1 green felt

Poinsettia Vest

Poinsettia Vest

Large Leaf
Cut 8 green felt

Gingerbread Men Sweatshirt
Continued from page 25

Gingerbread Man
Cut 2 tan felt

Quilted Holiday Cards

By Connie Ark

Give quilted holiday greeting cards to special friends this year. Use Christmas colors for a holiday card, or use traditional colors and make a card that can be used all year long.

Specifications

Skill Level: Beginner

Card Size: 8 1/2" x 11"

Materials

12" x 14" muslin or print for backing

1/4 yard sky fabric for background

1/8 yard snow/ground fabric

Scraps of blue/green (for blue spruce) or red/green (for pine tree) and brown and tan prints

Batting 10" x 12"

Embellishments: bangles, beads or buttons

6-strand green (for blue spruce) or red (for pine tree) embroidery floss

8" (3/16") dowel rod

1/2 yard 1/4"-wide ribbon

Basic sewing supplies and tools and washable fabric markers

Instructions

Step 1. Prepare templates using pattern pieces given. Cut as directed on each piece using either the blue/green or the red/green color combinations for tree color.

Step 2. Referring to Figure 1, join A triangles to make a tree shape; press. Sew B and BR to pieced tree section.

Sew C to D to C for base. Sew to bottom of the A-B section.

Step 3. Cut one piece tan scrap 2 3/4" x 9" and one piece background 2 1/4" x 9". Sew the tan piece to the bottom and the background piece to the top of the pieced section, again referring to Figure 1.

Step 4. Mark the words onto the top and bottom strips using patterns given for letters and a washable fabric marker.

Step 5. Using 2 strands of either red or green embroidery floss and a straight stitch, stitch letters onto top and bottom of pieced section.

Step 6. Place backing piece right side down on a flat surface. Center batting piece on top of backing. Place pieced section on top of batting.

Step 7. Quilt around tree shape and as desired by hand or machine.

Step 8. Trim batting edge even with front edge. Trim backing piece 3/4" larger all around. Turn under edge of backing 1/4". Fold remaining edge to front of quilted piece. Hand-stitch in place to finish edges, inserting small dowel through top edge before stitching.

Step 9. Embellish tree with floss bows, bangles or other trims as desried.

Step 10. Attach ends of ribbon to top backside for hanging.

Blue Spruce Holiday Card
Placement Diagram
8 1/2" x 11"

Pine Tree Holiday Card
Placement Diagram
8 1/2" x 11"

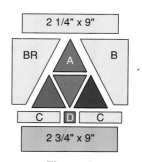

Figure 1
Join pieces as shown.

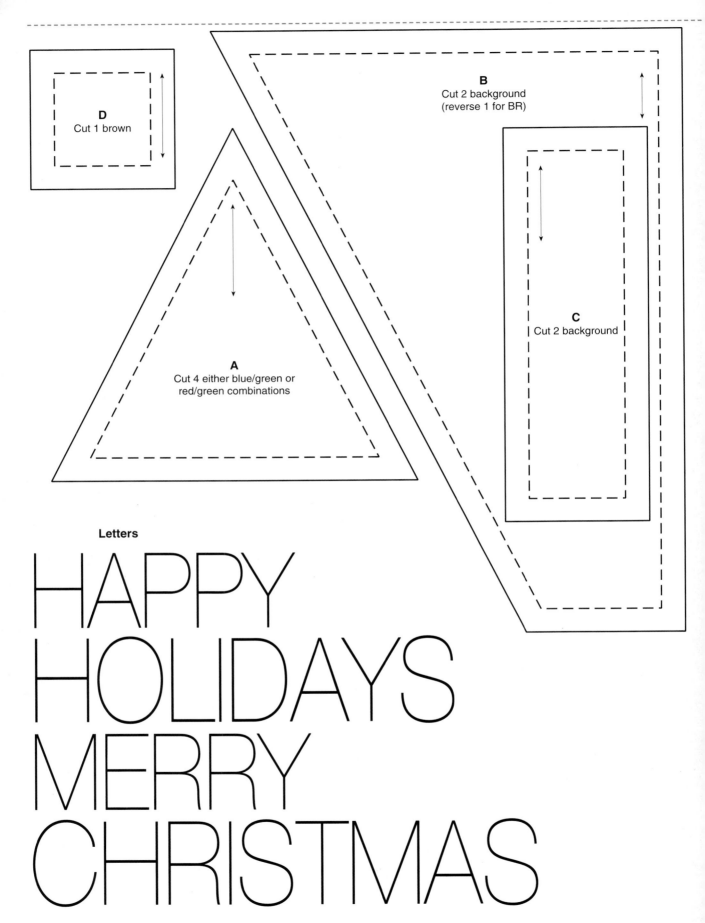

D
Cut 1 brown

B
Cut 2 background
(reverse 1 for BR)

C
Cut 2 background

A
Cut 4 either blue/green or
red/green combinations

Letters

HAPPY
HOLIDAYS
MERRY
CHRISTMAS

Home for Christmas Banner

By Anita Murphy

I made this small Christmas tree banner for my dear Aunt Helen. There wasn't much space in her room at the nursing home, but this little tree added some cheer during the holiday season. You, too, can be at home for Christmas no matter where you are with one of these little tree banners.

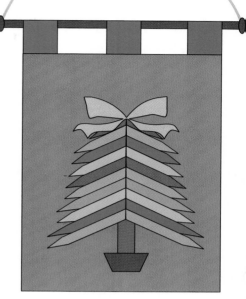

Home for Christmas
Placement Diagram
14 1/2" x 18 1/2"

Specifications

Skill Level: Beginner

Banner Size: 14 1/2" x 18 1/2"

Materials

5" x 6" scrap brown print

2 1/2" x 4" scrap brown solid

10 assorted Christmas green prints or solids ranging in size from 1 1/2"–2 1/2" wide to 6"–12" in length

15" x 19" background fabric

1/2 yard green solid for backing and loops

Batting 15" x 19"

Small amount of fiberfill

3/4 yard gold lace

1/2 yard gold cording

2 yards piping to match backing

3/8" x 20" dowel

2 (3/8") fancy wooden knobs

8–10 gold charms

All-purpose thread to match fabrics

Basic sewing supplies and tools

Instructions

Step 1. Prepare template for piece A; cut as directed on piece.

Step 2. Fold and crease background fabric to mark center.

Step 3. Fold the 2 1/2" x 4" brown solid trunk piece along length with right sides together. Stitch along raw edge using a small seam. Press with seam in center back. Center 3" up from the bottom edge of the background piece using crease as a guide. Hand-stitch in place with matching thread.

Step 4. Place two A pieces right sides together; sew around all four sides. Clip seams; trim corners. Cut a 1" slit in one layer of this piece using small, sharp scissors. Turn right side out through slit; press. Center A unit at the base of the tree trunk, covering raw edges at bottom of trunk piece. Hand-appliqué in place using matching thread.

Step 5. To make tree branches, cut green scrap pieces into several lengths ranging from 5 1/2"–10". You will need 20 strips—two of each fabric in the same size. Fold one strip right sides together; stitch one end closed at an angle as shown in Figure 1; trim. Turn right side out, stuff lightly in tip.

Step 6. Pin the stuffed tip about 1 1/2" from the side edge of the

Figure 1
Stitch 1 end at an angle.

background piece and 4 1/4" from the bottom. Pin the bottom side of fabric strip to curve up to cover the top of the trunk piece approximately 6" from bottom. Stitch to background fabric ending at center crease and leaving stitched tip free as shown in Figure 2. Fold under at center; trim excess.

Figure 2
Place first branch leaving stitched end free.

Step 7. Repeat for another strip of the same size and fabric for opposite side of tree. Sew this strip to the right side of the tree trunk making sure fabric meets and covers the center of the tree trunk.

Step 8. Lay a strip of fiberfill stuffing inside both tree branches as shown in Figure 3. Fold strips up as shown in Figure 4; do not turn under the raw edge as this will be the stitching line for the next branch.

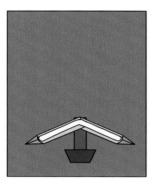

Figure 3
Place fiberfill inside strips.

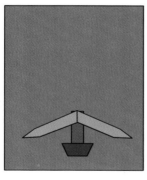

Figure 4
Fold strip up to
enclose fiberfill.

Step 9. Repeat for remaining branches, cutting each piece about 1/2" shorter than the previous one to make the tree narrower at the top. To sew next branch to background, lay

the lower part of the branch with right sides together and raw edges even with previously stitched branch; stitch. Fold up and stuff as before. Repeat for opposite side until there are 10 rows of stuffed branches. They should end about 3 1/2" from top edge of background piece. Fold under top edge of last strip; hand-stitch to background.

Step 10. Pin piping around outside edge of background piece, leaving 1" free at the beginning. Sew all around using a zipper foot on the machine. When getting close to the 1" tail, cut piping so that it will overlap slightly. Trim the cording from both ends to make the cording in both ends meet exactly as shown in Figure 5. Fold over raw edge of beginning end; stitch.

Figure 5
Cut cording where ends meet.

Step 11. Cut backing piece 15" x 19"; set aside. Cut a strip of backing fabric 6" x 15". Fold in half with right sides together along length. Sew along the long edge using a 1/4" seam allowance. Turn right side out; press with seam in the center.

Step 12. Cut strip into three 5" lengths. Fold each length in half with seam inside; pin in place at top of banner with raw edges even to make hanging tabs.

Step 13. Place backing piece right sides together with top piece; place batting underneath top piece. Stitch around outside edges on piping stitching line, leaving a 3" opening on bottom. Clip corners; turn right side out through opening. Hand-stitch opening closed.

Step 14. Stitch charms on tree branches as desired. Tie a bow with the gold lace; tack to top of tree. Insert dowel rod through loops. Place a drop of glue inside wooden knobs. Feed the cording inside the knobs; insert the dowel; let dry before hanging.

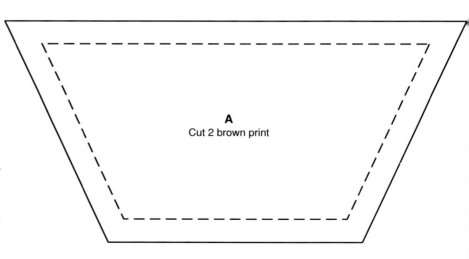

A
Cut 2 brown print

Holly Berry Santa Wall Quilt

By Christine Schultz

Hand appliqué and easy machine piecing combine to make this cheerful Christmas wall quilt showing Santa relaxing. His bag is full and he is ready to make his yearly trip in celebration of Christmas.

Specifications

Skill Level: Intermediate

Wall Quilt Size: 28 1/2" x 28 1/2"

Materials

3/4 yard background fabric

1/2 yard red print

1/3 yard green plaid

1/8 yard medium-dark plaid or print

Fabric scraps in various colors for face, fur, mitten, boot and toy sack

Backing 31" x 31"

Batting 31" x 31"

6-strand black embroidery floss

32 (1/4") red ball buttons

2 (3/8") black buttons

All-purpose thread to match fabrics

Basic sewing supplies and tools, freezer paper and washout marker

Instructions

Step 1. Wash and press all fabrics.

Step 2. Cut a piece of medium-dark plaid or print 3 1/2" x 13 1/2". Cut a piece of background fabric 10 1/2" x 13 1/2". Sew the 3 1/2" piece to the 10 1/2" piece along the 13 1/2" side; press.

Step 3. Trace pattern shapes on dull side of freezer paper using full-size pattern to make each shape. *Note: Shapes are reversed to make Santa face in the same direction as stitched sample.* Cut out shapes on the lines.

Step 4. Iron freezer paper shapes onto the wrong side of the appliqué fabrics. Cut out shapes leaving a 1/8"–1/4" turn-under seam allowance when cutting.

Step 5. Trace the full-size design onto the pieced background block using the washout marker and placing centering line on center of background on seam line between the two stitched pieces.

Step 6. Press seams of appliqué pieces to the wrong side on the freezer paper. Appliqué patches in place in numerical order as indicated on the full-size drawing using matching thread.

Step 7. Cut slits behind each appliqué shape; remove freezer paper through slits using tweezers, if necessary.

Step 8. Cut four strips green plaid 3/4" x 12 1/2". Cut 48 squares green plaid 2 1/2" x 2 1/2".

Step 9. From background fabric cut 96 squares 1 1/2" x 1 1/2"; four rec-

tangles 1 1/2" x 2 3/4"; four rectangles 1 1/2" x 2 1/2"; and four squares 4 3/4" x 4 3/4".

Step 10. For each holly leaf, fold or mark a diagonal line across the back of each 1 1/2" x 1 1/2" square. Lay this square on one corner of a green plaid square right sides together; sew on folded diagonal line as shown in Figure 1. Trim away corner as shown in Figure 2. Repeat on the opposite corner to complete one holly leaf unit as shown in Figure 3; repeat for 48 units.

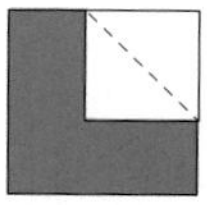

Figure 1
Sew on the diagonal of the square.

Figure 2
Trim off beyond seam.

Figure 3
Complete 1 holly leaf unit as shown.

Figure 4
Join 6 units to make a strip.

Step 11. Join six holly leaf units to make a leaf strip as shown in Figure 4; repeat for eight strips.

Step 12. Sew a 3/4" x 12 1/2" green plaid strip to one long side of one strip as shown in Figure 5. Sew a 1 1/2" x 2 3/4" background rectangle to one end of this stitched unit referring to Figure 6.

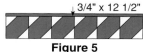

3/4" x 12 1/2"

Figure 5
Sew a 3/4" x 12 1/2" green plaid strip to 1 unit.

1 1/2" x 2 3/4"

Figure 6
Sew a 1 1/2" x 2 3/4" background rectangle to 1 end of a pieced unit.

Step 13. Sew a 1 1/2" x 2 1/2" background rectangle to one end of another pieced holly strip as shown in Figure 7.

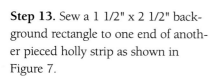

Figure 7
Sew a 1 1/2" x 2 1/2" background rectangle to 1 end of the pieced unit.

Step 14. Join the two pieced units as shown in Figure 8; repeat for four pieced holly leaf strips.

Figure 8
Join the 2 pieced units to make a holly leaf strip.

Step 15. Sew a holly strip to opposite long sides of quilt center; press seams toward strips.

Sew a 4 3/4" x 4 3/4" background square to each end of the remaining of strips. Sew strips to top and bottom; press seams toward strips.

Step 16. Cut two strips background 1 1/2" x 22"; sew to top and bottom of center piece. Cut two more strips 1 1/2" x 24"; sew to opposite long sides. Press seams toward strips.

Step 17. Cut two strips red print 3" x 24"; sew a strip to the top and bottom of the center piece. Cut two more strips 3" x 29"; sew

to opposite long sides. Press seams toward strips.

Step 18. Mark the bow quilting design on red border strips using pattern given and a washout marker.

Step 19. Using 3 strands black embroidery floss, make a French-knot eye on Santa as indicated on pattern. Sew red buttons in place on holly-leaf strips referring to Placement Diagram and photo of project for positioning.

Step 20. Quilt and finish quilt referring to General Instructions. Bind edges with self-made or purchased binding.

Bow Quilting Design

2

Center of corner

1

4

3

Match numbers to make complete pattern.

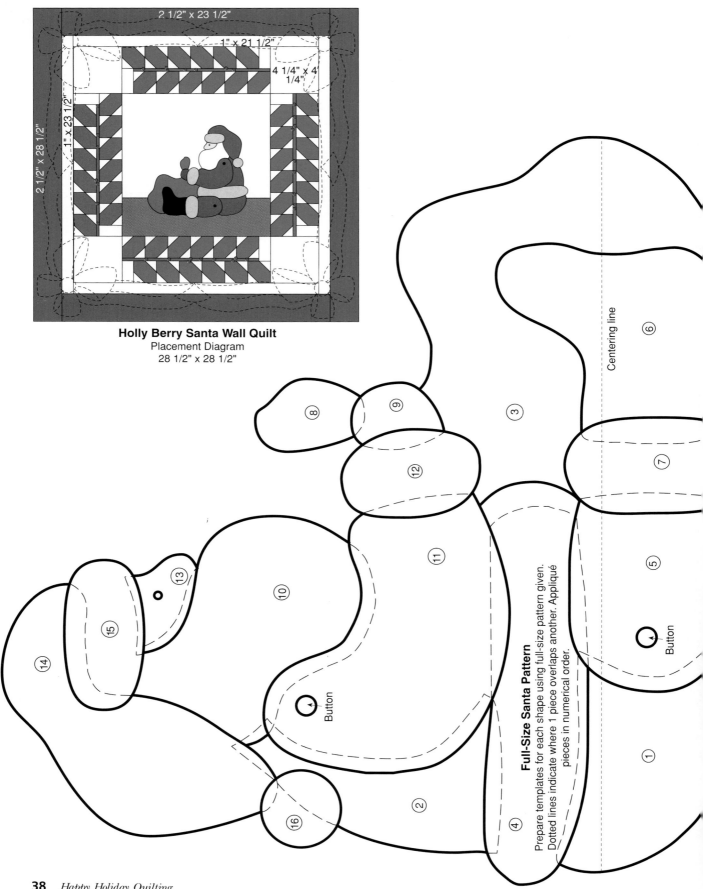

Holly Berry Santa Wall Quilt
Placement Diagram
28 1/2" x 28 1/2"

2 1/2" x 23 1/2"

1" x 21 1/2"

4 1/4" x 4 1/4"

1" x 23 1/2"

2 1/2" x 28 1/2"

Centering line

Button

Button

Full-Size Santa Pattern
Prepare templates for each shape using full-size pattern given.
Dotted lines indicate where 1 piece overlaps another. Appliqué
pieces in numerical order.

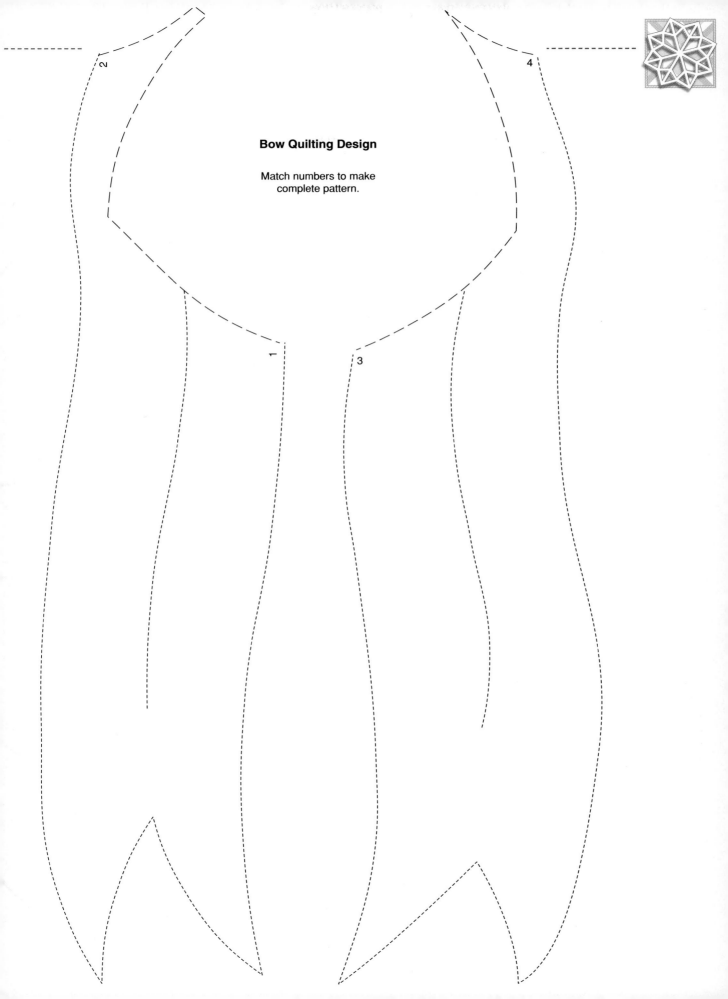

Bow Quilting Design

Match numbers to make
complete pattern.

2

4

1

3

2

4

Hanukkah Star Quilt

By Ann Boyce

Hanukkah, is an eight-day Jewish celebration. A gift is given to each family member on each of the eight days. The traditional colors for this December holiday are blue, gold and white and are represented in this wall quilt to honor the occasion.

Hanukkah Star
10" x 11 1/2" Block

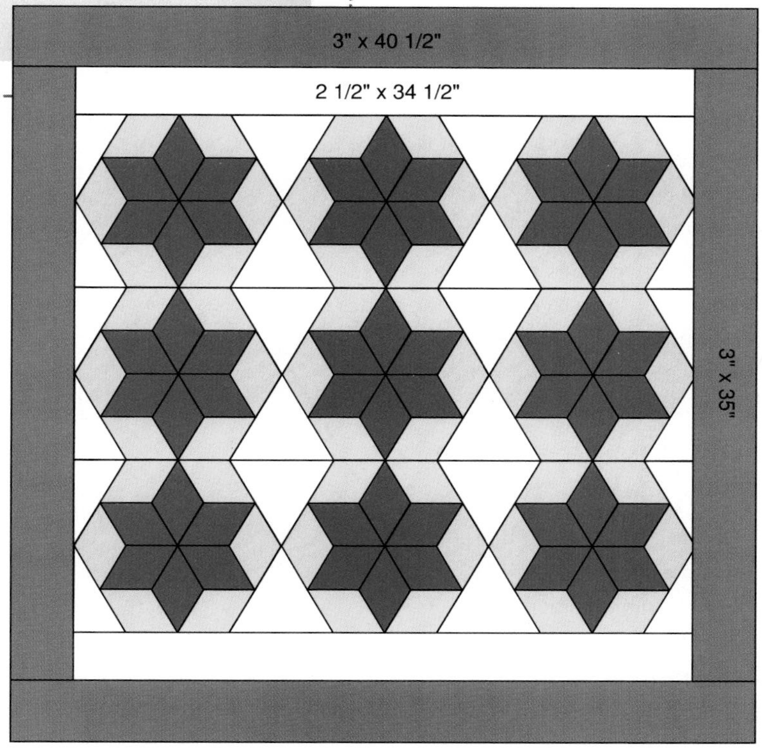

Specifications
Skill Level: Beginner

Wall Quilt Size: 40 1/2" x 41"

Block Size: 10" x 11 1/2"

Number of Blocks: 9

Materials
1/2 yard blue novelty print

1 yard white tone-on-tone print

1/2 yard each blue and gold tone-on-tone prints

Backing 45" x 45"

Batting 45" x 45"

Neutral color all-purpose thread

1 spool clear nylon monofilament

4 3/4 yards self-made or purchased binding

Basic sewing supplies and tools

Hanukkah Star
Placement Diagram
40 1/2" x 41"

Instructions

Step 1. Prepare templates using pattern pieces given. Cut as directed on each piece.

Step 2. Sew six blue A pieces together, stitching only seam lines to make star shape as shown in Figure 1. Set in and stitch gold A pieces between points as shown in Figure 2. Repeat for nine blocks.

Step 3. Sew C and CR to one side of

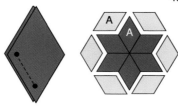

Figure 1
Join pieces, starting and stopping stitching on seam line only.

Figure 2
Set in gold A pieces.

six blocks as shown in Figure 3. Join three blocks with four B pieces to

make a row as shown in Figure 4; repeat for three rows; join rows and press.

Step 4. Cut two strips white tone-on-tone print 3" x 35". Sew a strip

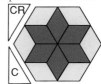

Figure 3
Sew C and CR to 1 side of 6 blocks.

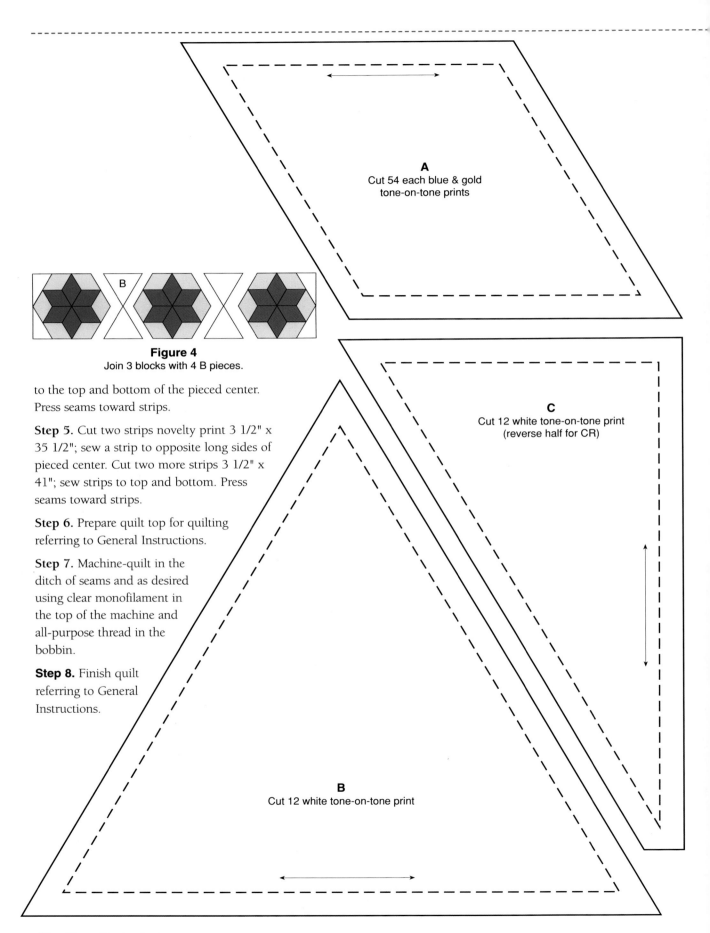

A
Cut 54 each blue & gold
tone-on-tone prints

Figure 4
Join 3 blocks with 4 B pieces.

to the top and bottom of the pieced center. Press seams toward strips.

Step 5. Cut two strips novelty print 3 1/2" x 35 1/2"; sew a strip to opposite long sides of pieced center. Cut two more strips 3 1/2" x 41"; sew strips to top and bottom. Press seams toward strips.

Step 6. Prepare quilt top for quilting referring to General Instructions.

Step 7. Machine-quilt in the ditch of seams and as desired using clear monofilament in the top of the machine and all-purpose thread in the bobbin.

Step 8. Finish quilt referring to General Instructions.

C
Cut 12 white tone-on-tone print
(reverse half for CR)

B
Cut 12 white tone-on-tone print

Sweetheart Roses

By Jill Reber

The tradition of receiving roses for Valentine's Day is long-lived. You will give your favorite sweetheart a dozen roses that will last forever when you make this charming wall quilt.

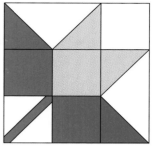

Sweetheart Rose
6" x 6" Block

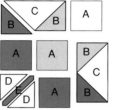

Figure 1
Join units to
complete 1 block.

Figure 2
Join units to
complete
corner block.

Specifications
Skill Level: Intermediate

Wall Quilt Size: 28" x 34"

Block Size: 6" x 6"

Number of Blocks: 12

Materials
1/4 yard each 3 different rose prints for flowers

1/2 yard dark green solid for stems and binding

1/3 yard green print for leaves

3/4 yard light print for background

3/4 yard floral print for outside borders

Backing 32" x 38"

Batting 32" x 38"

1 spool each off-white, rose and dark green quilting thread

Neutral color all-purpose thread

Basic sewing supplies and tools and Master Piece 45 ruler

Project Notes
The Master Piece 45 ruler was used to construct the project shown. You may purchase this ruler at your local quilt shop, use templates given or cut using strip-method instructions given.

Traditional Method
Step 1. Prepare templates using pattern pieces given. Cut as directed on each piece. *Note: Follow directions given in the package for using Master Piece 45 ruler, if you choose to use it rather than templates or strip-cutting methods.*

Step 2. Referring to Figure 1 to piece one block, sew a rose print B to a background C to a green print B; repeat reversing placement of B colors. Sew a rose print A to a green print A. Sew a background D to each long side of E; sew to a green print A. Sew a background A to the rose end of one B-C-B unit. Arrange pieced units and join to complete one block; repeat for 12 blocks. Press all blocks.

Step 3. Arrange the blocks in four rows of three blocks each. Join blocks in rows; join rows. Press pieced center.

Step 4. Cut two strips background 1 1/2" x 18 1/2"; sew to top and bottom. Cut two strips background 1 1/2" x 26 1/2"; sew to opposite long sides. Press seams toward border strips.

Step 5. To piece corner blocks, sew a background B to a rose print B; repeat. Sew rose print side of one unit to a rose print A. Sew rose print side of one unit to a background A. Join these two units as shown in Figure 2 to complete one corner block; press. Repeat for four blocks.

Step 6. Cut two strips floral print 4 1/2" x 20 1/2"; sew to top and bottom. Cut two strips floral print 4 1/2" x 26 1/2". Sew a corner square to each end of each strip referring to the Placement Diagram for positioning of blocks. Sew a strip to opposite long sides; press seams toward strips.

Step 7. Prepare top for quilting referring to General Instructions.

Step 8. Quilt as desired by hand or machine using off-white quilting thread on background and borders, green quilting thread on green print pieces and rose quilting thread on rose print pieces. When quilting is complete, trim edges even. Prepare self-made binding and finish referring to General Instructions.

Quick Method
Step 1. Cut one strip from each rose print 2 7/8" by fabric width. Cut eight 2 7/8" segments from each rose print strip. Trim remaining strips to 2 1/2" wide. Cut four 2 1/2" segments from two rose prints and eight from one rose print for A squares.

Step 2. Cut each 2 7/8" x 2 7/8" square in half on one diagonal to make B triangles. *Note: You will have extra triangles of these colors.*

Step 3. Cut one strip dark green solid 3 1/2" x 10 1/2". Cut strip into 7/8" x 3 1/2" rectangles for E stem pieces, or use E templates; you will need 12 E pieces.

Step 4. Cut one strip green print 2 7/8" by fabric width. Cut strips into 2

7/8" segments; repeat for 12 segments. Cut each segment in half on the diagonal to make 24 B triangles.

Step 5. Cut two strips green print 2 1/2" by fabric width. Cut into 2 1/2" segments; repeat for 24 segments for A.

Step 6. Cut two strips background 2 5/8" by fabric width. Cut strips into 2 5/8" segments; cut in half on one diagonal to make D triangles. Repeat for 24 triangles.

Step 7. Cut four 2 7/8" x 2 7/8" squares background. Cut each square in half on one diagonal for B triangles.

Step 8. Cut six squares background 5 1/4" x 5 1/4". Cut each square in half on both diagonals for C triangles.

Step 9. Cut one strip background 2 1/2" by fabric width. Cut into 2 1/2" segments for A; you will need 16 A squares.

Step 10. Join pieces as for traditional method referring to Figure 1 to complete blocks.

Step 11. Piece corner blocks as for traditional method referring to Figure 2.

Step 12. Complete project referring to Traditional Method Steps 3–9 to complete project.

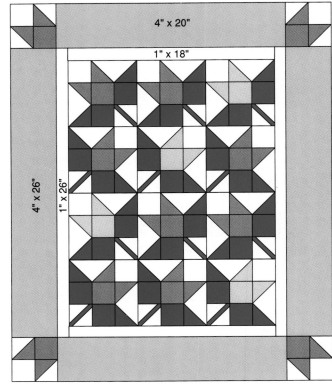

Sweetheart Rose
Placement Diagram
28" x 34"

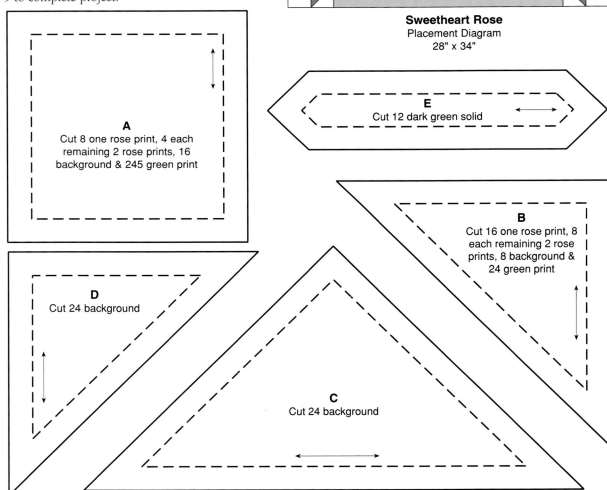

A
Cut 8 one rose print, 4 each remaining 2 rose prints, 16 background & 245 green print

E
Cut 12 dark green solid

B
Cut 16 one rose print, 8 each remaining 2 rose prints, 8 background & 24 green print

D
Cut 24 background

C
Cut 24 background

Spring Flings

*S*pring is full of special occasions to gather
with family and friends. In this chapter, you'll
find wall quilts for St. Patrick's Day, Easter, May
Day, Arbor Day, Mother's Day and even National
Pig Day! Celebrate a new birth with teddy bear bibs
and a matching wall quilt. Enjoy the colors of
spring as you celebrate this time of year.

Decorate your quilting room or home office with
this lovely coordinated set that includes a wall quilt, pen
and pencil box (or quilt supply box), picture frame,
chair cushion and desk pad/calendar holder. You'll want
to quilt additional sets to give for Mother's Day or
Secretary's Day or as a special gift for your quilting friends.
Flowers at the Office pattern begins on page 48.

Flowers at the Office

By Connie Rand

These days many people work from their home offices. Since quilters are always looking for ways to use their talents to decorate their homes, there's no reason to leave out the office. Why not make your workspace extra-special with these paper-pieced floral accessories?

Specifications

Skill Level: Intermediate

Pencil Box Size: 4" x 4" x 4"

Picture Frame Size: 15 1/2" x 17 1/2"

Chair Cushion Size: 16" x 16"

Wall Quilt Size: 22" x 22"

Desk Pad Holder Size: 21" x 30"

Block Size: 4" x 4"

Number of Blocks: 11 for all projects

Materials

3 yards green print

3/4 yard purple print

1/4 yard blue print

1/2 yard yellow print

1/2 yard cream-on-cream print

Scraps of magenta and pink prints

1 sheet mat board or cardboard 32" x 40" and one sheet 16" x 20"

Batting 45" x 60"

Neutral color all-purpose thread

4 1/2 yards self-made or purchased binding for chair cushion and 2 1/2 yards for wall quilt

Basic sewing tools and supplies

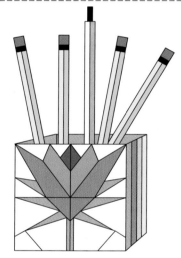

Pen & Pencil Box
Placement Diagram
4" x 4" x 4"

Piecing Blocks

Step 1. Copy or trace full-size sections for paper-piecing pattern. *Note: Fabric pieces will be placed on the front of the pattern; sewing will be done on the back of the pattern. If the pattern lines are not visible on the back, trace the lines on the back of the paper as guides for placement.*

Step 2. Set sewing machine for 16–18 stitches per inch. Cut each scrap of fabric at least 1/4" larger on all sides than each area.

Step 3. Beginning with Section 1 piece 1, place a small green print

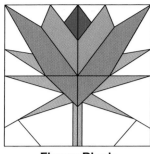

Flower Block
4" x 4" Block

scrap on the front of the pattern over area 1. Place a piece of cream-on-cream print to fit area 2 over the green print, right sides together. Sew along the 1–2 line on the back of the pattern beginning two stitches before the line and extending into the seam allowance area.

Step 4. Turn pattern over; trim seam allowance to 1/8"–1/4". Flip the cream piece over to cover area 2; press seam.

Step 5. Continue adding pieces in numerical order using fabric colors as shown in colored drawing and Placement Diagram to complete Section 1; repeat for Sections 2–6. Trim the completed sections along the outer seam allowance lines; leave paper pattern intact. Join sections as shown in Figure 1 to complete one block. Repeat for 11 blocks; square up to 4 1/2" x 4 1/2".

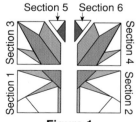

Figure 1
Join sections as shown to complete Flower block.

Pen & Pencil Box

Step 1. Cut one strip each 1 1/2" by fabric width green, purple, blue and yellow prints. Sew together in the

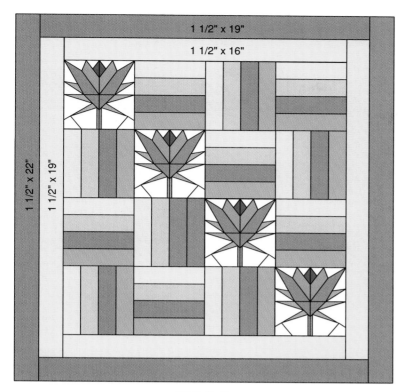

Wall Quilt
Placement Diagram
22" x 22"

order shown in Figure 2; cut into 4 1/2" segments. You will need three segments. Set aside remainder of strips for another project.

Step 2. Join one pieced Flower block with the three strip-pieced segments as shown in Figure 3.

Step 3. Cut batting and backing 4 1/2" x 16 1/2". Place pieced unit on top of batting. Machine-quilt along strips as shown in Figure 4.

Figure 2
Sew 1 1/2" strips together in color order shown; cut in 4 1/2" segments.

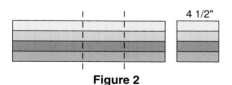

Figure 3
Join Flower block with strip-pieced segments to make box sides as shown.

Step 4. Place backing and quilted unit right sides together; sew together along three edges as shown in Figure 5. Turn right side out; machine-quilt through all layers as shown in Figure 6, stopping 1/4" from bottom edge.

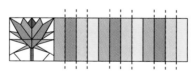

Figure 4
Machine-quilt box as shown.

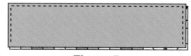

Figure 5
Sew pieced unit and backing together as shown.

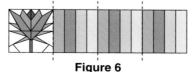

Figure 6
Machine-quilt through all layers as shown.

Step 5. For bottom, cut two squares green print and one square batting 4 1/2" x 4 1/2". Place green print squares right sides together on top of batting; sew around three edges through all layers. Turn right side out.

Step 6. Cut five pieces mat board or heavy cardboard 3 7/8" x 3 7/8". Slip one piece into each of the pockets formed in Steps 4 and 5. Turn raw edges in; slipstitch openings closed.

Step 7. Bring ends of box together to form a square as shown in Figure 7; slipstitch ends together. Slipstitch bottom onto box to finish.

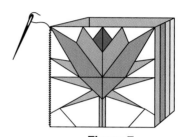

Figure 7
Slipstitch edges of box together as shown

Wall Quilt

Step 1. Cut one strip each 1 1/2" by fabric width from green, purple, blue and yellow prints. Sew together in the order shown in Figure 2; cut into 4 1/2" segments. You will need 12 segments.

Step 2 Using four of the previously pieced Flower blocks, sew strip segments together with blocks in rows as shown in Figure 8. Join rows to complete pieced center.

Step 3. Cut two strips yellow print 2" x 16 1/2"; sew to top and bottom of pieced center. Cut two more strips yellow print 2" x 19 1/2"; sew a strip to opposite sides of pieced center. Press seams toward strips.

Step 4. Cut two strips purple print 2" x 19 1/2"; sew to top and bottom of pieced center. Cut two more strips purple print 2" x 22 1/2"; sew to opposite sides of pieced center. Press seams toward strips.

Step 5. Finish wall quilt referring to General Instructions.

Figure 8
Join strip segments and Flower blocks together in rows as shown.

Picture Frame

Project Note

This frame is made to hold an 8" x 10" photograph. Be creative and adjust the frame to fit your needs. The block and borders could be reduced in size to make a different size frame. Also, the Flower block could be turned to make a horizontal frame. If you wish, make four Flower blocks, placing one in each corner, adjusting green print strips to fit.

Step 1. Cut two 4 1/2" x 10", one 4 1/2" x 12" and one 4 1/2" x 16" green print rectangles. Sew the rectangles together with one previously pieced Flower block as shown in Figure 9, leaving center open.

Step 2. Cut three pieces green print and two pieces batting 16" x 18". Set aside two green print rectangles and one batting piece for back of frame. Layer one green print piece with remaining batting piece; baste together.

Step 3. Lay front of frame on top of basted green print/batting rectangle. Stitch around center of frame 1/4" from edge of inside frame front as shown in Figure 10. Trim backing away along inside edges of frame front. Clip corners; turn right side out.

Step 4. Press stitched edge lightly. Baste layers together. Quilt at 1" intervals as shown in Figure 11.

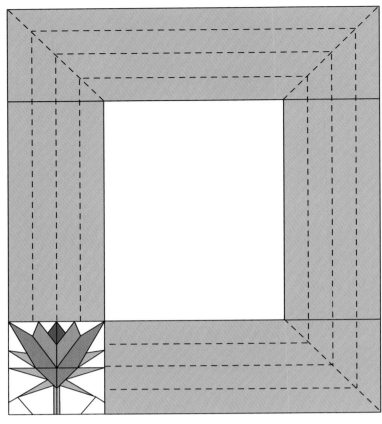

Picture Frame
Placement Diagram
15 1/2" x 17 1/2"

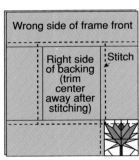

Figure 10
Stitch around center of frame 1/4" from edge of inside frame front as shown.

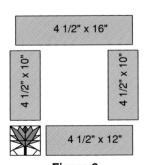

Figure 9
Sew green print rectangles and Flower block together as shown to make front of frame.

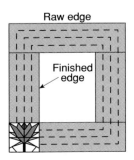

Figure 11
Quilt at 1" intervals as shown.

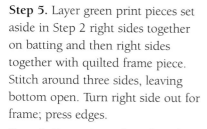
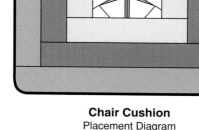
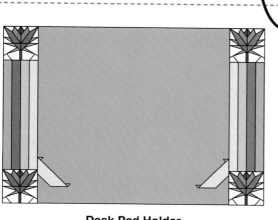
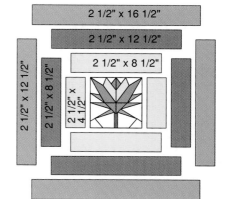

Desk Pad Holder
Placement Diagram
21" x 30"

Chair Cushion
Placement Diagram
16" x 16"

Step 5. Layer green print pieces set aside in Step 2 right sides together on batting and then right sides together with quilted frame piece. Stitch around three sides, leaving bottom open. Turn right side out for frame; press edges.

Step 6. Cut a piece of mat board or heavy cardboard 15 3/8" x 17 3/8". Slip this into the opening in the bottom of the frame; slipstitch opening closed. Add a sleeve or plastic rings to the back for hanging if desired.

Step 7. Slide 8" x 10" photograph through front opening; position picture so it is centered in the frame. Carefully lift up frame front securing edges of picture inside frame using glue stick.

Desk Pad Holder

Project Note

This desk pad holder is made to hold a 22" x 17" desk pad. Adjust project measurements if desk pad used is of a different size.

Step 1. Cut one strip each 1 1/2" by fabric width from blue, green, purple and yellow prints. Sew these strips together in the order shown in Figure 2. Cut two strip sets 13 1/2" long. Sew one previously pieced Flower block to each end of each strip.

Step 2. Cut two pieces each green

print and batting 4 1/2" x 21 1/2". Lay pieced section face up on batting.

Step 3. Machine-quilt along length of strips and across top and bottom of strips. Place backing piece on top of the quilted top piece right sides together; sew around three sides. Turn right side out for side units.

Step 4. Cut two pieces of mat board or heavy cardboard 3 7/8" x 20 7/8" and insert into side units through open side. *Note: If the mat board or cardboard doesn't slide in easily, try rounding the top corners a little or trimming the sides slightly.* Turn raw edges of side unit under; slipstitch closed.

Step 5. Cut two pieces green print for backing and one batting 21 1/2" x 30 1/2", and one piece of mat board or heavy cardboard 21" x 30". Layer green pieces right sides together on batting. Stitch around three sides; turn right side out and press. Insert mat board or cardboard through opening and turn raw edges under; slipstitch opening closed.

Step 6. Lay side units on top of completed back piece, aligning outside edges; slipstitch around all outside edges. Place purchased 17" x 22" desk pad in center.

Step 7. Cut two strips yellow print 2 1/2" x 6". Fold in half wrong sides together along length; stitch along long edge. Turn right side out. Place desk pad on project and position strips on bottom corners as shown on the Placement Diagram. Remove desk pad and hand-sew ends in place to finish. *Note: When desk pad is in use, the ends of these strips will not be visible, but will help to hold desk pad in place.*

Chair Cushion

Step 1. Cut two strips each yellow print 2 1/2" x 4 1/2" and 2 1/2" x 8 1/2", two strips each purple print 2 1/2" x 8 1/2" and 2 1/2" x 12 1/2"

2 1/2" x 16 1/2"

2 1/2" x 12 1/2"

2 1/2" x 8 1/2"

2 1/2" x 12 1/2"

2 1/2" x 8 1/2"

2 1/2" x 4 1/2"

Figure 12
Sew strips to Flower block as shown to make cushion front.

and two strips each green print
2 1/2" x 12 1/2" and 2 1/2" x 16 1/2".

Step 2. Using one of the previously
pieced Flower blocks, sew strips cut
in Step 1 around block sewing shorter strips of each color to opposite
sides and longer strips of each color
to top and bottom referring to Figure
12. Press all seams toward strips.

Step 3. Cut one piece green print and
two pieces batting 16 1/2" x 16 1/2".

Step 4. Layer pieced front with green
print backing piece and batting.
Machine-quilt around center block
and around each set of strips. Baste
outside raw edges together. Round
corners, if desired.

Step 5. Bind edges referring to
General Instructions and as follows:
Cut one piece binding 48" long; set
aside. Bind three edges of cushion
with remaining piece of binding,
leaving an 18" tail at beginning and

end of stitching for ties; trim any
excess beyond 18". Center and pin
48" length of binding to the remaining side of the cushion. Stitch to
cushion as before, leaving tails for
ties. Press and stitch to finish ties.
Hand-stitch binding to backside of
cushion to finish.

Step 6. Fold tail pieces in 1/4" to
wrong side on each raw edge; fold
along length with wrong sides
together, turning ends under.

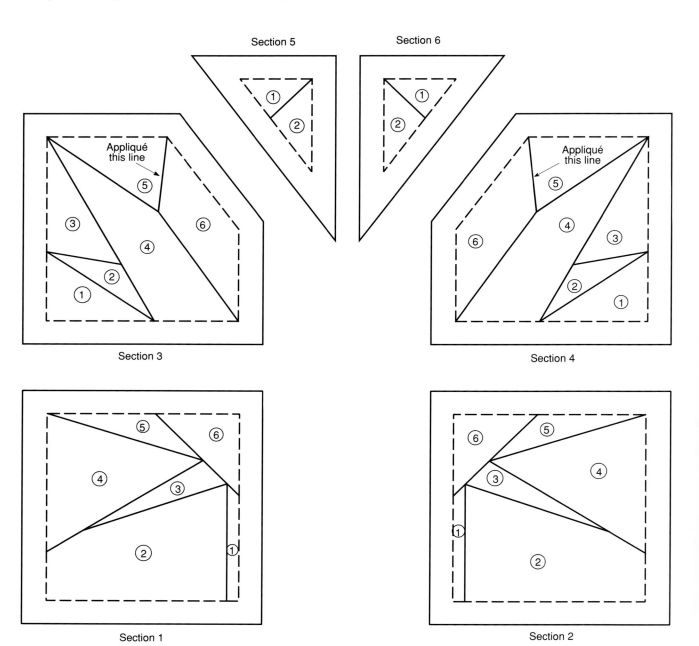

Piggy Parade

By Norma Storm

Make this wall quilt with little piglets following their mother, and be ready for National Pig Day on March 1.

Piggy Parade
Placement Diagram
18" x 35"

Specifications

Skill Level: Intermediate

Wall Quilt Size: 18" x 35"

Materials

1/2 yard yellow solid for background

Fat quarter pink tone-on-tone print

1/8 yard green print

Scraps pink prints 4" x 4"

1/8 yard black solid

1/2 yard pig print

Backing 21" x 38"

Batting 21" x 38"

All-purpose thread to match fabrics

6-strand pink embroidery floss

Permanent black fabric marker

Basic sewing supplies and tools

Instructions

Step 1. Cut pieces for all sections, adding 1/4" seam allowance to each piece when cutting or copy pattern and use as paper-piecing pattern referring to General Instructions for paper-piecing directions. *Note: Patterns are reversed for paper piecing.*

Step 2. Cut as directed on each piece for color. Stitch pieces together in numerical order in sections. Join sections to complete pieced unit as shown in Figure 6, appliquéing curve of pig's head in section 1 and underside of pig in section 3.

Step 3. Cut one piece green print 1 1/8" x 12 1/2". Sew strip to bottom of pieced section; press.

Step 4. Cut one strip green print 1 5/8" x 16 1/2" and one piece yellow 9 7/8" x 16 1/2". Sew the two strips together to complete second section of pieced center. Sew to pieced Pig unit as shown in Figure 7; press.

Step 5. Arrange baby pigs on pieced center referring to Placement Diagram. Hand-appliqué in place.

Step 6. Draw eyes, mouth and hooves using black permanent fabric marker and as indicated on pattern pieces.

Step 7. Using 3 strands pink embroidery floss, stem-stitch tails on pigs.

Step 8. Cut two strips black solid 1" x 28 1/2"; sew to top and bottom of pieced section. Press seams toward strips. Cut two more strips black solid 1" x 12"; sew to short sides of pieced section. Press seams toward strips.

Step 9. Cut two strips pig print 3 1/2" x 29 1/2"; sew to top and bottom of pieced section. Press seams toward strips. Cut two more strips pig print 3 1/2" x 18; sew to short sides of pieced section. Press seams toward strips.

Step 10. Referring to the photograph for suggestions, mark quilting designs on completed top.

Step 11. Finish quilt as desired referring to General Instructions. *Note: The quilt shown was finished stitching backing fabric right sides together with layered top and batting, leaving an opening. Then it was turned right side out through opening. The opening was hand-stitched closed and the project quilted by machine to finish.*

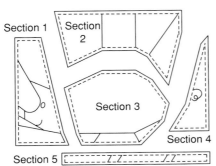

Figure 6
Join 5 pieced sections to complete pieced pig unit.

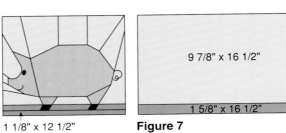

9 7/8" x 16 1/2"

1 5/8" x 16 1/2"

1 1/8" x 12 1/2"

Figure 7
Join pieced units as shown.

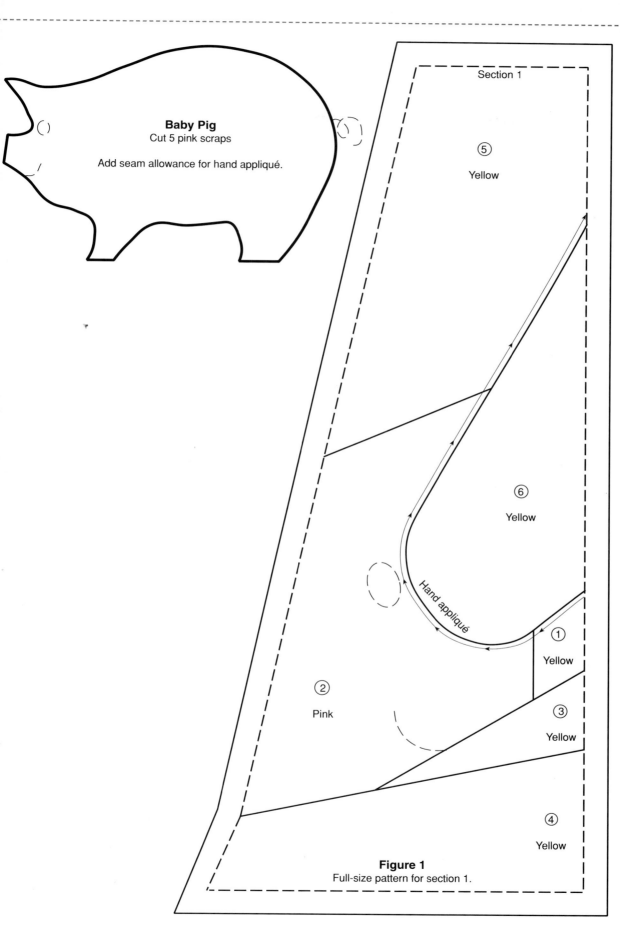

Baby Pig
Cut 5 pink scraps

Add seam allowance for hand appliqué.

Section 1

⑤
Yellow

⑥
Yellow

Hand appliqué

① Yellow

② Pink

③ Yellow

④ Yellow

Figure 1
Full-size pattern for section 1.

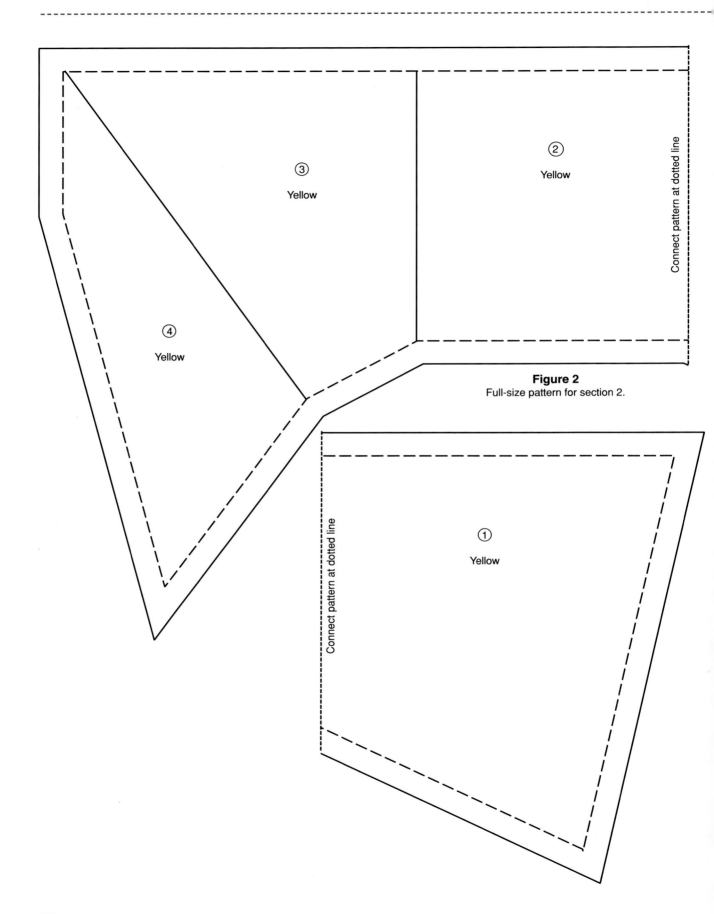

③ Yellow

② Yellow

Connect pattern at dotted line

④ Yellow

Figure 2
Full-size pattern for section 2.

Connect pattern at dotted line

① Yellow

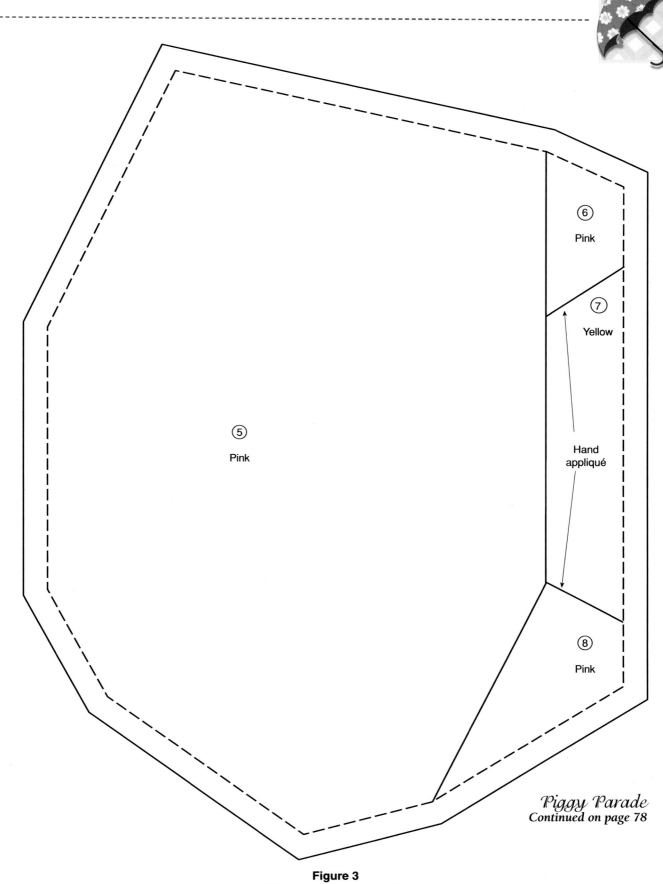

⑥

Pink

⑦

Yellow

Hand
appliqué

⑤

Pink

⑧

Pink

Piggy Parade
Continued on page 78

Figure 3
Full-size pattern for section 3.

Lucky Shamrocks

By Diana DiPaolo

Celebrate Saint Patrick's Day with this Double Irish Chain wall quilt. The luck of the Irish will be with you as you quilt this Irish treasure.

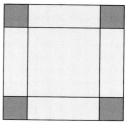

Block 1
7 1/2" x 7 1/2"

Block 2
7 1/2" x 7 1/2"

Specifications

Skill Level: Beginner

Wall Quilt Size: 31 1/2" x 31 1/2"

Block Size: 7 1/2" x 7 1/2"

Number of Blocks: 9

Materials

3/4 yard each light and dark prints

1 yard medium print

Backing 35" x 35"

Batting 35" x 35"

Neutral color all-purpose thread

1 spool green quilting thread

3 3/4 yards self-made or purchased binding

Basic sewing supplies and tools

Instructions

Step 1. Cut the following strips in sizes given: light print—one strip 2" by fabric width, two strips 5" x 22" and four strips 2" x 22"; medium print—four strips 2" x 22" and five strips 2" by fabric width; and dark print—four strips 2" by fabric width and one strip 2" x 22".

Step 2. Join two dark, two medium and one light 2" by fabric width strips together along length to make A segments. Cut stitched section in 2" segments referring to Figure 1; you will need 10 A segments.

Step 3. Sew three medium and two dark 2" by fabric width strips together along length to make B segments. Cut stitched section in 2" segments referring to Figure 2; you will need 10 B segments.

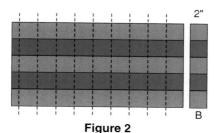

2"

Figure 2
Cut ten 2" segments for B as shown.

Step 4. Sew two light, two medium and one dark 2" x 22" fabric strips together along length to make C segments. Cut stitched section in 2" segments referring to Figure 3; you will need five C segments.

Step 5. Arrange two A, two B and one C segment together in rows referring to Figure 4; join rows to complete Block 1; repeat for five blocks. Press and square up to 8" x 8".

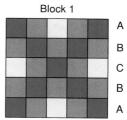

Block 1

A
B
C
B
A

Figure 4
Join A, B and C segments to make Block 1.

Step 6. Sew one light 5" x 22" strip between two medium 2" x 22" strips together along length to make D segments. Cut stitched section in 2" segments referring to Figure 5; you will need eight D segments.

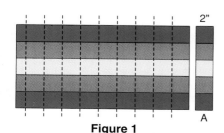

2"

Figure 1
Cut ten 2" segments for A as shown.

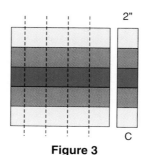

2"

Figure 3
Cut five 2" segments for C as shown.

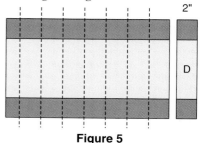

2"

D

Figure 5
Cut eight 2" segments for D as shown.

Step 7. Sew one light 5" x 22" strip between two light 2" x 22" strips along length to make E segments. Cut stitched section in 5" segments referring to Figure 6; you will need four E segments.

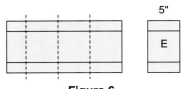

Figure 6
Cut four 5" segments for E as shown.

Step 8. Sew two D segments to each E segment to make Block 2 as shown in Figure 7; repeat for four blocks. Press and square up to 8" x 8".

Block 2

Figure 7
Join E and D segments to make Block 2 as shown.

Step 9. Arrange Blocks 1 and 2 in rows referring to Figure 8. Join in rows; join rows to complete pieced center; press.

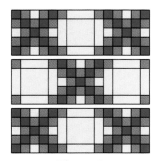

Figure 8
Arrange blocks in rows as shown.

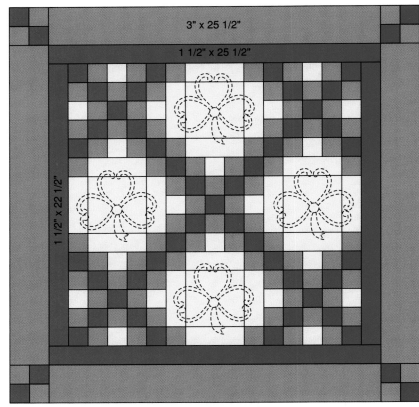

Lucky Shamrock
Placement Diagram
31 1/2" x 31 1/2"

Step 10. Cut two strips dark print 2" x 23"; sew a strip to opposite sides of pieced center. Press seams toward strips. Cut two strips dark print 2" x 26"; sew a strip to remaining opposite sides. Press seams toward strips.

Step 11. Using leftover 2" x 2" pieces, create four Four-Patch squares for corners referring to Figure 9.

Figure 9
Make Four-Patch corner blocks as shown.

Step 12. Cut four strips medium print 3 1/2" x 26"; sew a strip to opposite sides of pieced center. Press seams toward strips. Sew a Four-Patch square to each end of the remaining two strips. Sew a strip to remaining opposite sides; press seams toward strips.

Step 13. Mark quilting design given in the center of the light print squares referring to Placement Diagram and project for positioning.

Step 14. Finish quilt as desired referring to General Instructions.

Quilting Design
Place on block using dotted
lines marked around design.

Stained-Glass Cross

By Holly Daniels

Make this colorful banner to hang in a prominent location in your home during the Easter season. Its bright and cheerful colors are a reminder of the reasons Christians celebrate Easter.

Cross Block
7" x 7"

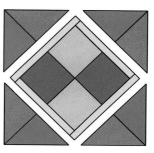

Figure 3
Sew a triangle unit to each side of the bordered Four-Patch unit.

Specifications

Skill Level: Intermediate

Banner Size: Approximately 21 3/4" x 36 1/2" (without binding)

Block Size: 7" x 7"

Number of Blocks: 7

Materials

1/8 yard each pink, green, light blue and peach hand-dyed or purchased solids

1/4 yard yellow hand-dyed or purchased solid

Backing 24" x 40"

Low-loft batting 24" x 40"

Neutral color all-purpose thread

3 1/2 yards self-made or purchased binding

24" length 1/4" wood dowel

Basic sewing tools and supplies

Instructions

Step 1. Cut one strip each peach and blue 2 5/8" by fabric width. Cut each strip in 2 5/8" squares; you will need 14 squares each color.

Step 2. Sew a blue square to a peach square; repeat for 14 sets. Sew pairs together to form a Four-Patch unit as shown in Figure 1; repeat for seven units.

Step 3. Cut three strips 7/8" by fabric width yellow. Cut strips into fourteen 4 3/4" segments and fourteen 5 1/2" segments. Sew a 4 3/4" segment to two opposite sides of each Four-Patch unit. Sew a 5 1/2" segment to the remaining opposite sides of the Four-Patch unit; press seams toward segments. Repeat for all Four-Patch units.

Figure 1
Join squares to make Four-Patch units.

Step 4. Cut seven squares each pink and green 4 3/4" x 4 3/4". Cut each square in half on both diagonals to make triangles.

Step 5. Sew a green triangle to a pink triangle as shown in Figure 2; repeat for 28 units.

Step 6. Sew a triangle unit to each side of the pieced and bordered Four-

Figure 2
Join triangles as shown.

Patch units as shown in Figure 3; press seams toward pieced triangles.

Step 7. Cut six strips yellow 7/8" x 7 1/2". Join five blocks with four strips as shown in Figure 4.

Step 8. Sew a 7/8" x 7 1/2" yellow strip to one side of the two remaining pieced blocks as shown in Figure 5. Sew the bordered side of each block to opposite sides of the second block from the top as shown in Figure 6; press completed top.

7/8" x 7 1/2"

Figure 4
Join 5 blocks with 4 strips.

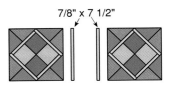

Figure 5
Sew a 7/8" x 7 1/2" yellow strip to
1 side of 2 blocks as shown.

Figure 6
Sew a block to each side of
second block as shown.

Step 9. Prepare top for quilting referring to General Instructions. *Note:
Batting and backing should be trimmed
to fit cross shape before quilting.*

Step 10. Quilt as desired and bind
edges referring to General
Instructions.

Step 11. Cut three strips any remaining fabric 4" x 7". Fold each 4" end
on each piece in 1/4"; press and
stitch. Fold each piece right sides
together along length. Sew to make a
tube. Turn right side out; press seam
in center.

Step 12. Hand-stitch the tubes on
the backside of the pieced cross referring to Figure 7 for placement.

Step 13. Cut a 5 1/2" piece from 24"
length of dowel. Insert 5 1/2" piece
in top sleeve and remaining long
piece through both sleeve openings
on cross piece on backside to hang.

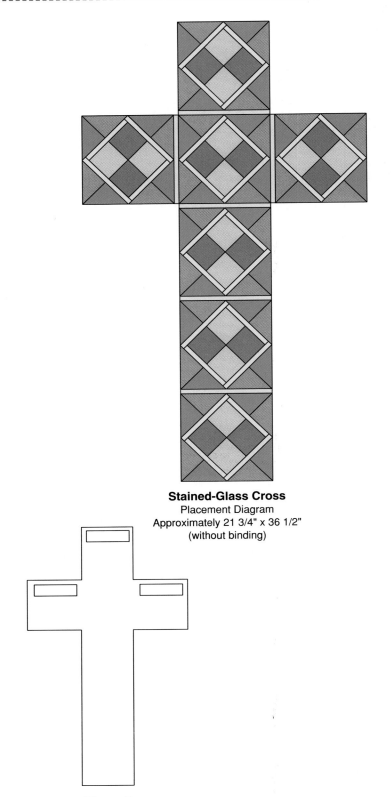

Stained-Glass Cross
Placement Diagram
Approximately 21 3/4" x 36 1/2"
(without binding)

Figure 7
Place tubes on backside of pieced
cross for hanging as shown.

Bunnies in a Basket

By Diana DiPaolo

This friendly bunny is checking to see if the time is right to come out and greet all the children waiting for the arrival of the Easter Bunny.

Bunnies in a Basket
6 1/2" x 7 1/2" Block

Specifications

Skill Level: Intermediate

Wall Quilt Size: 25" x 27"

Block Size: 6 1/2" x 7 1/2"

Number of Blocks: 4

Materials

1/4 yard yellow pin dot

1/2 yard each basket print and purple tone-on-tone print

1/8 yard white felt

Backing 28" x 30"

Batting 28" x 30"

All-purpose thread to match fabrics

3 yards self-made or purchased binding

Freezer paper

1/2 yard fusible transfer web

Make-up blusher

Black permanent marker

Basic sewing supplies and tools

Instructions

Step 1. Trace head, ear and paw shapes onto paper side of fusible transfer web referring to each pattern shape for number to trace. Cut around shapes, leaving space between. Fuse shapes onto felt. Cut out shapes on traced lines; remove paper backing.

Step 2. Trace head, ear and arc stencils onto paper side of freezer paper referring to each pattern shape for number to trace. Cut out shapes on traced line. Iron shiny side down onto the felt side of the head and ears. *Note: These pieces will be used as stencils for coloring.*

Step 3. Cut a strip purple 4 3/4" by fabric width. Cut strip into four 7" x 4 3/4" and two 4 1/2" x 4 1/2" segments. Cut four strips purple 1 1/4" by fabric width. Cut strips into eight 1 1/4" x 8" and eight 1 1/4" x 8 1/2" segments.

Step 4. For handles, cut one strip 12" by fabric width from basket print. Cut one square 12" x 12" from strip; cut square in half on one diagonal to make two triangles. Place triangles right sides together; cut three 1"-wide

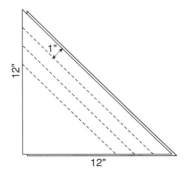

Figure 1
Cut strips across diagonal
of triangles to make bias
strips for handles.

bias strips across diagonal as shown in Figure 1. Fold under both long edges of each strip a scant 1/4"; press. Set aside.

Step 5. From remaining basket fabric, cut one 7 3/4" x 7 3/4" square and two 4 1/2" x 4 1/2" squares. Cut the larger square in half on both diagonals to make four triangles.

Step 6. From yellow pin dot fabric, cut three strips 1 1/2" by fabric width. Cut strips into three 1 1/2" x 19 1/2" and six 1 1/2" x 9" segments.

Step 7. Place one freezer paper head pattern on a white felt head piece. Use black permanent marker to color in eyes in freezer-paper openings as shown in Figure 2; repeat for all heads. Placing one freezer paper ear pattern on each felt ear, color open area with make-up blusher to make pink sections on ears; remove freezer paper.

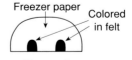

Figure 2
Press freezer paper on
white felt; color in eyes.

Step 8. Place freezer-paper arc on the 4 3/4" x 7" purple background

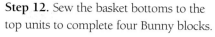

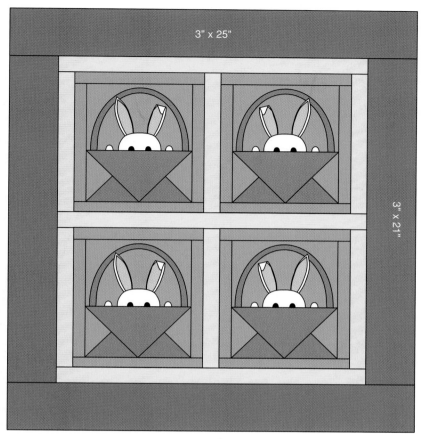

Bunnies in a Basket
Placement Diagram
25" x 27"

basket bottoms as shown in Figure 5; repeat for four basket bottoms.

Step 12. Sew the basket bottoms to the top units to complete four Bunny blocks.

Step 13. Sew a 1 1/4" x 8" purple background strip to opposite sides of each Bunny block. Sew a 1 1/4" x 8 1/2" purple background strip to top and bottom of each Bunny block. Press seams toward strips.

Step 14. Join two blocks with three 1 1/2" x 9 1/2" yellow pin dot strips to make a row; repeat for two rows. Join two rows with three 1 1/2" x 19 1/2" yellow pin dot strips as shown in Figure 6.

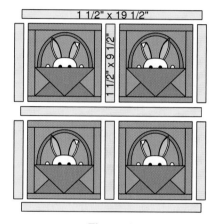

Figure 6
Join block rows with yellow pin dot strips.

Step 15. Cut two strips Easter print 3 1/2" x 21 1/2"; sew to opposite sides of pieced center. Cut two more strips 3 1/2" x 25 1/2"; sew to top and bottom of pieced center. Press seams toward strips.

Step 16. Fold one ear on each block down referring to the photo of the project. Place pressing cloth over unpressed sections of each ear; press in place.

Step 17. Finish quilt as desired referring to General Instructions. *Note: The quilt shown was finished by stitching backing fabric right sides together with layered top and batting, leaving an opening. Then it was turned right side out through opening. The opening was hand-stitched closed and the project quilted by machine.*

piece. Using the freezer paper as a guide, stitch a folded bias strip to the background fabric along pressed line by hand or machine. Remove freezer paper; press handle piece back and blind-stitch in place.

Step 9. Press bunny heads and paws to purple background under handle, tucking ears under head as marked on pattern piece for location. Leave tip of one ear unpressed to fold down, referring to the Placement Diagram; repeat for four top units.

Step 10. Place the 4 1/2" x 4 1/2" squares of basket and background fabric right sides together; cut on both diagonals as shown in Figure 3. Stitch triangles together as shown in Figure 4.

Step 11. Sew one of the pieced triangles to the short sides of the large triangle previously cut in Step 5 to make

4 1/2"

4 1/2"

Figure 3
Cut 4 1/2" squares in half on both diagonals as shown.

Make 1

Make 1

Figure 4
Join triangles as shown.

Figure 5
Sew triangle sets to short sides of a large triangle.

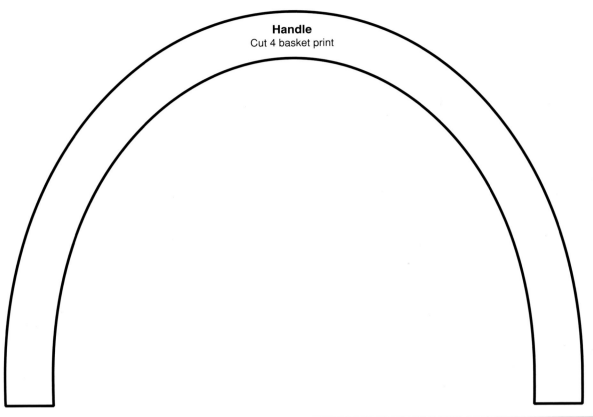

Handle
Cut 4 basket print

Arc Stencil
Cut 4 freezer paper

Head Stencil
Cut 4 freezer paper

Paw
Cut 8 white felt

Ear Stencil
Cut 8 freezer paper
(reverse half)

Ear
Cut 4 white felt

Ear

Ear

Head
Cut 4 white felt

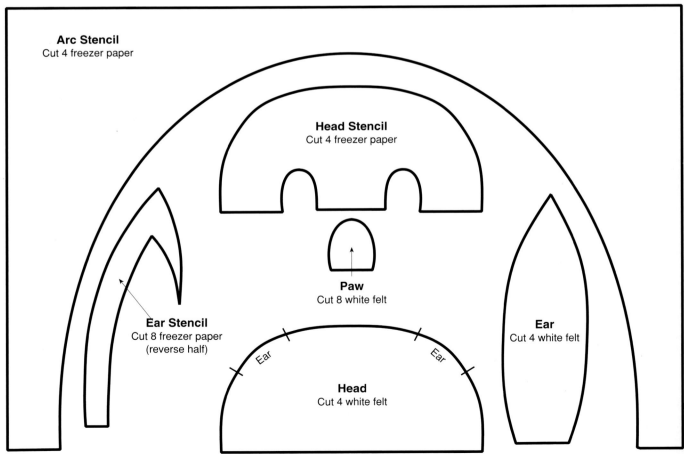

Mother's Day Basket

By Janice McKee

Fill this quilted basket with favorite bath supplies, jewelry, makeup or stationery for a lovely Mother's Day gift.

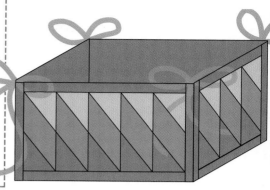

Mother's Day Basket
Placement Diagram
Approximately 6 3/4" x 10 3/4" x 4 3/4"

Specifications

Skill Level: Intermediate

Quilted Basket Size:
Approximately 6 3/4" x 10 3/4" x 4 3/4"

Materials

3/4 yard pink print

1/8 yard each light pink and medium pink solids

20" x 40" piece thin batting

All-purpose thread to match fabrics

Stiff cardboard such as mat board

3 yards 3/8"-wide pink satin ribbon

Basic sewing tools and supplies, glue and masking tape

Instructions

Step 1. Cut the following from cardboard or mat board: one piece 6 3/4" x 10 3/4" cardboard for basket bottom; two pieces 4 3/4" x 10 3/4" for front and back pieces; and two pieces 4 3/4" x 6 3/4" for ends.

Step 2. Cut two pieces batting using basket bottom measurement. Glue batting to both sides of bottom. Cut two pieces batting each for sides and ends of basket using measurements given in Step 1 for each piece. Glue batting to inside of corresponding cardboard pieces.

Step 3. Prepare templates using pattern pieces given. Cut as directed on each piece.

Step 4. Sew a medium pink solid A to B to a light pink solid A to make one unit as shown in Figure 1; repeat for 16 units.

Figure 1
Sew A to B to A as shown.

Step 5. Join three units as shown in Figure 2 for end piece; repeat for two end pieces.

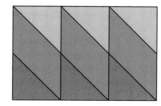

Figure 2
Join 3 units for end sections.

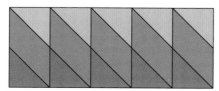

Figure 3
Join 5 units for side sections.

Step 6. Join five units as shown in Figure 3 for side piece; repeat for two side pieces.

Step 7. Cut four strips 2" x 6 1/2" pink print; sew to opposite long sides of each end section. Cut four strips 2" x 7 1/2"; sew to remaining sides of each end section as shown in Figure 4.

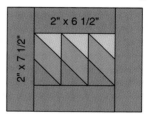

Figure 4
Sew strips to end sections.

Step 8. Cut four strips 2" x 10 1/2" pink print; sew to opposite long sides of each side section. Cut four strips 2" x 7 1/2"; sew to remaining sides of each side section as shown in Figure 5.

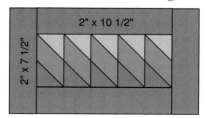

Figure 5
Sew strips to side sections.

Step 9. Cut pieces of batting and backing to extend 1" all around each pieced section. Layer and machine-quilt around each pink print A piece on all pieced sections.

Step 10. Trim batting and backing 1/4" larger all around than pieced sections without added strips. Fold the stitched strips at top and bottom of pieces over to the backing leaving 1/4" or more showing on right side; stitch in the ditch of the seam on the right side between strips and pieced sections to form top and bottom binding; repeat on ends of sections.

Step 11. From pink print, cut one piece 9" x 13" and one piece 7 1/4" x 11 1/4". Center basket bottom on top of wrong side of the larger rectangle. Fold the raw edges over on top of basket bottom; slipstitch to batting. Press under 1/4" all around on smaller rectangle. Pin in place as lining for basket bottom, covering raw edges; slipstitch in place to finish bottom piece.

Step 12. Cut pieces for lining for basket sides and ends in the same manner, with 1" of fabric extending every side of cardboard. Fold raw edges over on top of cardboard and use masking tape to hold in place. Line each piece using this method.

Step 13. Place pieced and quilted outside sections for sides and ends on top of their corresponding cardboard pieces; whipstitch together. Lay out pieces as shown in Figure 6; hand-stitch bottom of each piece to basket bottom.

Step 14. Cut eight 12" pieces of ribbon. Stitch securely to both sides of the top of each of the sides and ends of basket. Tie together to form basket.

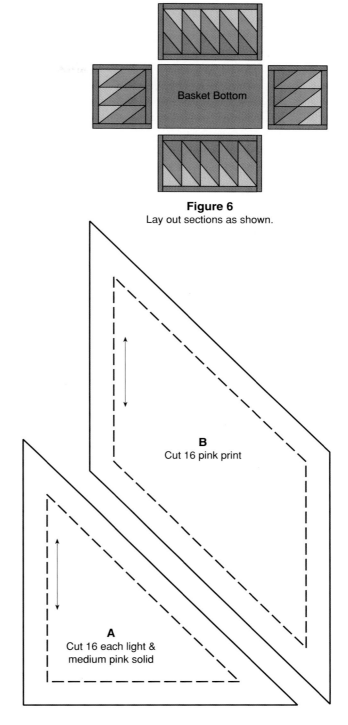

Figure 6
Lay out sections as shown.

B
Cut 16 pink print

A
Cut 16 each light &
medium pink solid

Bear Babies

By Marian Shenk

Make bibs and a matching wall banner to welcome Baby.
The three bear designs are sure to delight at mealtime.

Specifications

Skill Level: Beginner

Banner Size: 20" x 45"

Block Size: 11" x 11"

Number of Blocks: 3 for wall quilt

Materials

1/2 yard each white solid and blue and pink prints

1/8 yard yellow print

Scraps brown velour

Scraps pink, blue, yellow and green prints or solids

Backing 23" x 48"

Batting 23" x 48"

All-purpose thread to match fabrics

1 spool white quilting thread

Green, yellow, pink, brown, red and black 6-strand embroidery floss

3 3/4 yards self-made or purchased binding

Basic sewing tools and supplies, glue and masking tape

Bear Babies Wall Banner

Instructions

Step 1. Trace bear pattern pieces for each bear, marking detail lines as indicated by dotted lines on patterns. Cut pieces as directed on patterns, adding a 1/8" seam allowance to turn under for hand-appliqué.

Step 2. Cut three squares white solid 11 1/2" x 11 1/2". Fold and crease to mark center. Center bear designs on each square; pin or baste in place. Hand-appliqué pieces in place using matching thread.

Step 3. Using 2 strands brown floss, stem-stitch detail lines on each bear. Using 2 strands floss, on Hungry Bear stitch bows with pink and bib with blue and balloon strings on Balloon Bear with green, yellow and pink floss. Satin-stitch eyes with 2 strands black floss, noses with 2 strands brown floss and mouths with 2 strands red floss referring to Placement Diagrams, photo of projects and patterns for positioning and color.

Figure 1
Join blocks with strips as shown.

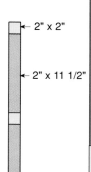

Figure 2
Sew squares to strips to make side border strip.

Bear Babies Wall Quilt
Placement Diagram
20" x 45"

Step 4. Cut 10 strips pink print 2" x 11 1/2". Join three blocks with four strips beginning and ending with a strip as shown in Figure 1; press seams toward strips.

Step 5. Cut eight squares yellow print 2" x 2". Join four squares with three pink strips to make side borders as shown in Figure 2. Sew one of these strips to each side of the previously pieced section; press seams toward strips.

Step 6. Cut four squares yellow print 3 1/2" x 3 1/2". Cut two strips blue print 3 1/2" x 14 1/2" and two strips 3 1/2" x 39 1/2". Sew the shorter strips to top and bottom; press seams toward strips.

Step 7. Sew a yellow square to each end of the remaining two strips. Sew these strips to long sides of pieced section; press seams toward strips.

Step 8. Mark quilting design given in blue border strips and diagonal lines spaced 1 1/4" apart on white background referring to Placement Diagram for positioning.

Step 9. Finish referring to the General Instructions.

Bear Baby Bibs

Project Specifications
Skill Level: Beginner
Bib Size: 10 1/2" x 12"

Materials
Scraps brown or tan velour

3/4 yard white flannel or terry cloth for tops and backing

Scraps blue, pink, green, yellow and pink solids or prints

14" x 36" piece batting

Neutral color all-purpose thread

1 spool white quilting thread

Green, yellow, pink, brown, red and black 6-strand embroidery floss

3 packages wide bias tape in choice of colors

Basic sewing tools and supplies

Instructions

Step 1. Prepare paper pattern using bib pattern given. Cut as directed on piece for one bib.

Step 2. Choose a bear pattern from the three patterns given. Prepare pattern, cut and appliqué design in the center of bib front as in wall banner.

Step 3. Stitch detail lines referring to wall banner instructions Step 3.

Step 4. Sandwich batting piece between appliquéd bib front and backing piece. Outline quilt 1/4" or more away from bear shape and as desired on bear.

Step 5. Bind around outside edges with purchased bias tape as shown in Figure 3; trim excess at ends. Turn binding to backside; hand-stitch in place. Bind across top edge, leaving at least 12" on each side of bib for ties as shown in Figure 4. Turn binding to backside; hand-stitch in place along bib section and machine-stitch folded edges beyond bib on tie ends to finish.

Step 6. Repeat to make one bib from each bear design.

Figure 3
Sew binding around outside edge as shown; trim excess at ends.

Figure 4
Sew binding across top edge, leaving at least 12" on each side for ties.

Balloon Bear
Placement Diagram
10 1/2" x 12"

Hungry Bear
Placement Diagram
10 1/2" x 12"

Sleepy Bear
Placement Diagram
10 1/2" x 12"

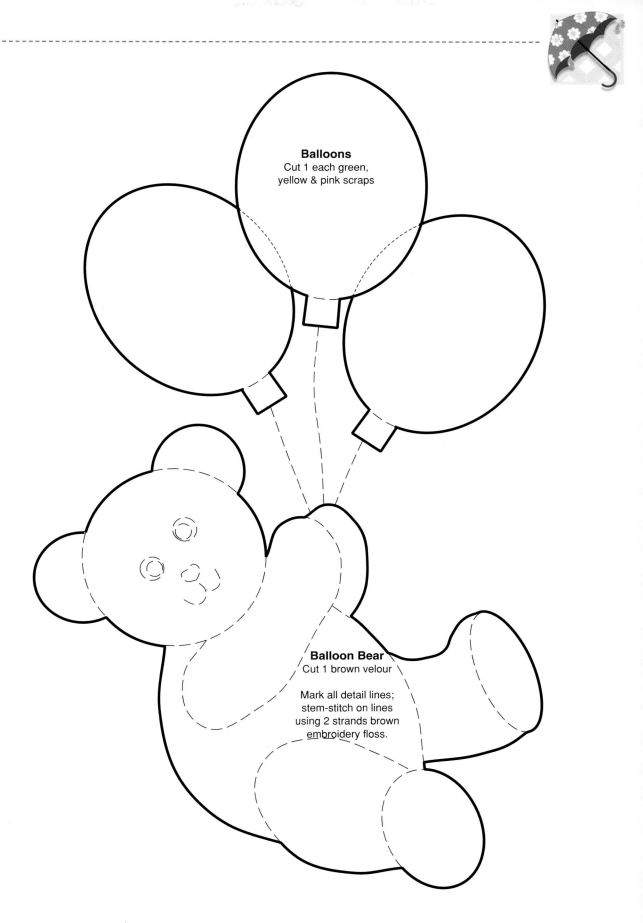

Balloons
Cut 1 each green,
yellow & pink scraps

Balloon Bear
Cut 1 brown velour

Mark all detail lines;
stem-stitch on lines
using 2 strands brown
embroidery floss.

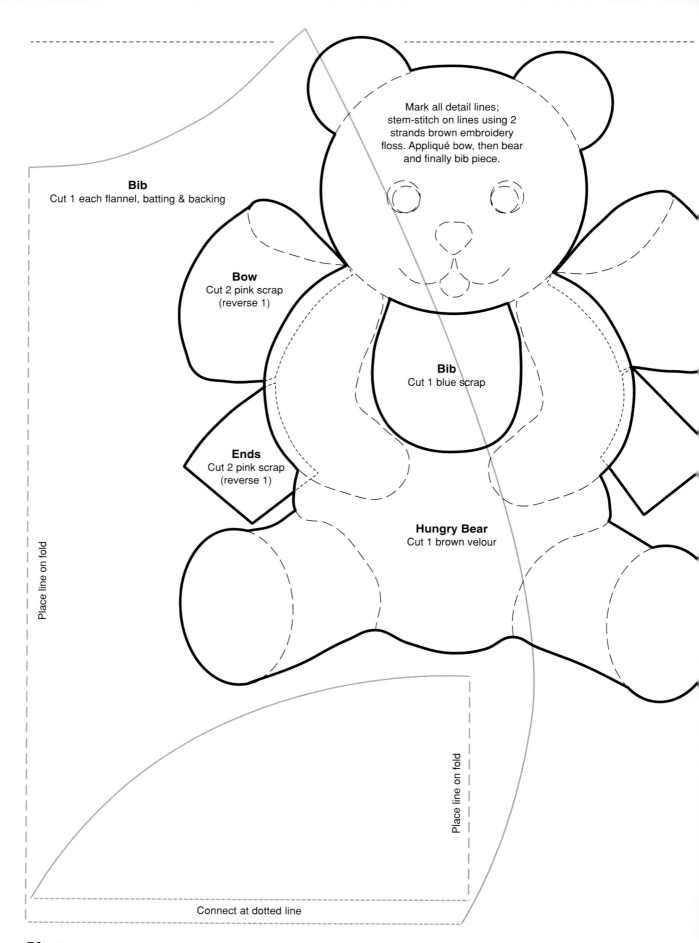

Bib
Cut 1 each flannel, batting & backing

Bow
Cut 2 pink scrap
(reverse 1)

Ends
Cut 2 pink scrap
(reverse 1)

Mark all detail lines;
stem-stitch on lines using 2
strands brown embroidery
floss. Appliqué bow, then bear
and finally bib piece.

Bib
Cut 1 blue scrap

Hungry Bear
Cut 1 brown velour

Place line on fold

Place line on fold

Connect at dotted line

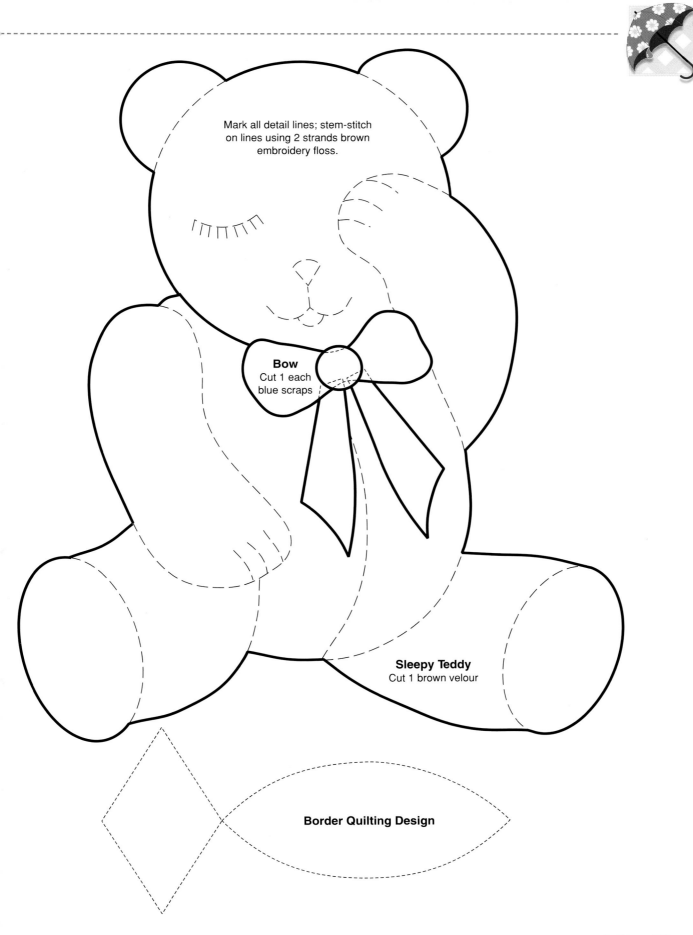

Mark all detail lines; stem-stitch
on lines using 2 strands brown
embroidery floss.

Bow
Cut 1 each
blue scraps

Sleepy Teddy
Cut 1 brown velour

Border Quilting Design

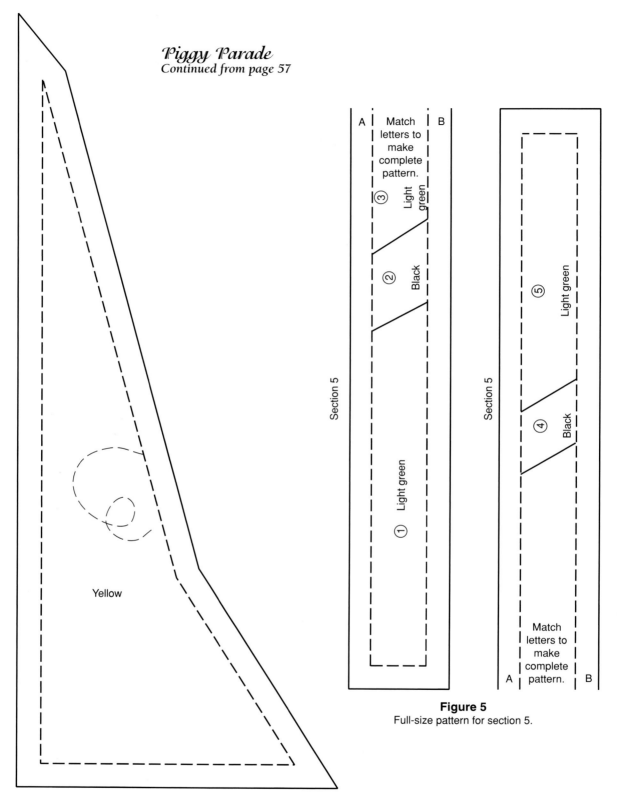

Piggy Parade
Continued from page 57

Figure 4
Full-size pattern for section 4.

Yellow

Section 5

A | Match letters to make complete pattern. | B

③ Light green

② Black

① Light green

Figure 5
Full-size pattern for section 5.

Section 5

⑤ Light green

④ Black

Match letters to make complete pattern.

A | | B

A Tree for All Seasons

By Sue Harvey

Celebrate Arbor Day by planting a table full of trees with this table topper and matching coaster set. The table topper could also be made into a wall quilt by turning the tree blocks to all point in one direction.

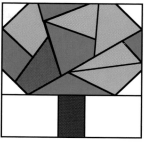

Maple Tree
4" x 4" Block

Specifications

Skill Level: Intermediate

Table Topper Size: 15 3/4" x 15 3/4"

Coaster Size: 4 1/2" x 4 1/2"

Block Size: 4" x 4" and 2" x 2"

Number of Blocks: 4 large; 4 small

Materials

1/8 yard each 13 assorted light, medium and dark green prints

1/2 yard dark green print

1/8 yard cream/green print

Scrap brown print

Fat quarter cream solid

1/2 yard batting

2 yards dark green self-made or purchased binding

All-purpose thread to match fabrics

Basic sewing supplies and tools and tracing paper

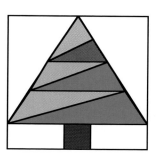

Pine Tree
4" x 4" Block

Coaster Set

Step 1. Copy or trace full-size paper-piecing pattern for each large tree. *Note: Fabric pieces will be placed on the front of the pattern; sewing will be done on the back of the pattern. If the pattern lines are not visible on the back, trace the lines on the back of the paper as guides*

for placement. Patterns are reversed for paper piecing when necessary.

Step 2. For each piece, cut a scrap of fabric at least 1/4" larger on all sides than each area. Set sewing machine for 16–18 stitches per inch.

Step 3. Beginning with the Spruce Tree Coaster pattern, place a small brown fabric scrap on the front of the pattern over area 1. Place a piece of cream fabric to fit area 2 over the brown, right sides together. Sew along the 1–2 line on the back of the pattern beginning two stitches before the line and extending into the seam allowance area.

Step 4. Turn pattern over; trim seam allowance to 1/8"–1/4". Flip the cream piece over to cover area 2; press.

Step 5. Continue adding pieces in numerical order using fabric colors as marked on pattern to complete the block. Trim the completed tree block along the outer seam allowance line; leave paper pattern intact.

Step 6. Repeat Steps 2–5 to make a Pine Tree Coaster block.

Step 7. Sew an Oak Tree Coaster block in two separate sections, referring to Steps 2–5. Trim each completed section along the outer seam allowance line. Combine the two sec-

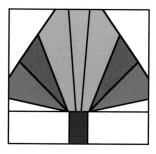

Oak Tree
4" x 4" Block

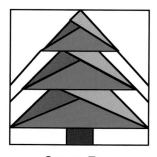

Spruce Tree
4" x 4" Block

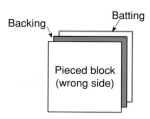

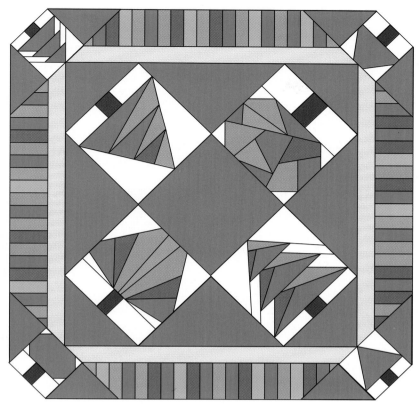

A Tree for All Seasons Table Topper
Placement Diagram
15 3/4" x 15 3/4"

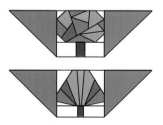

Backing

Batting

Pieced block
(wrong side)

Figure 3
Layer pieced block with batting
and backing as shown.

Step 11. Remove paper pattern. Turn right side out through opening; hand-stitch opening closed.

Step 12. Quilt as desired by hand or machine. Repeat for each tree block to complete four coasters.

Table Topper

Step 1. Follow Steps 1–8 of Coaster set instructions to make one of each large tree block. Repeat for one of each 2" tree blocks using patterns given.

Step 2. Cut two squares dark green print 5 3/8" x 5 3/8". Cut each square in half on one diagonal to make four half/square triangles. Sew one of these triangles to two opposite sides of the Maple Tree block and the Oak Tree block as shown in Figure 4; press seams toward triangles.

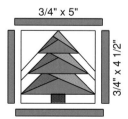

Figure 4
Sew a triangle to opposite sides
of the Maple Tree and Oak Tree
blocks as shown.

tions to complete the block. Press seam toward trunk section.

Step 8. Sew a Maple Tree Coaster block in four separate sections, referring to Steps 2–5. Trim each completed section along the outer seam allowance line. Combine sections 1 and 2 referring to Figure 1; press seam toward section 1. Combine this with section 3; press seam toward section 3. Combine this section with section 4; press seam toward section 4.

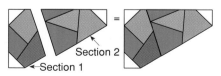

=

Section 2

Section 1

Figure 1
Join sections 1 and 2.

Step 9. Cut eight strips dark green print 3/4" x 4 1/2". Referring to Figure 2, sew a strip to two opposite sides of each pieced tree block; press

seams toward strips. Cut eight strips dark green print 3/4" x 5". Sew a strip to two remaining sides of each tree block. Press seams toward strips.

3/4" x 5"

3/4" x 4 1/2"

Figure 2
Sew border strips to each
tree block as shown.

Step 10. Cut four pieces each dark green print for backing and batting 5" x 5". Place one tree block right sides together with one backing piece; place a batting square under backing as shown in Figure 3. Sew around outside edge using a 1/4" seam allowance and leaving a 2" opening on one side.

Step 3. Cut one square dark green print 5 3/4" x 5 3/4". Cut the square in half on both diagonals as shown in Figure 5 to make four quarter-square triangles. Sew one of these to the bottom of each large tree block as shown in Figure 6; press seams toward triangles.

Step 4. Cut one square dark green print 4 1/2" x 4 1/2". Join the Pine

Tree and Spruce Tree blocks with the square as shown in Figure 7; press seams toward square.

Step 5. Sew the pieced Maple Tree and Oak Tree units to opposite sides of the Pine Tree and Spruce Tree unit as shown in Figure 8. Press seams away from center unit.

Step 6. Cut two strips cream/green print 1 1/4" x 12". Sew a strip to opposite sides of pieced center; press seams toward strips. Cut two strips

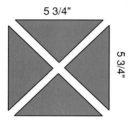

5 3/4"

5 3/4"

Figure 5
Cut square on both diagonals
to make a quarter-square
triangle as shown.

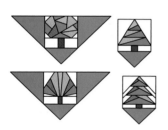

Figure 6
Sew a triangle to the bottom
of each tree block.

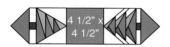

4 1/2" x
4 1/2"

Figure 7
Join the Pine Tree and Spruce
Tree blocks with the square.

Figure 8
Join the pieced units as shown.

cream/dark green print 1 1/4" x 13 1/2". Sew strips to remaining sides; press seams toward strips. *Note: Strips are longer than needed.*

Step 7. Cut 13 strips 1" x 16" from assorted light, medium and dark green prints. Sew the strips together on the 16" sides to make a pieced section. Press seams in one direction. Cut strips into eight 2" segments units as shown in Figure 9.

Step 8. Join two strip units on short ends to make one 2" x 13 1/2" border unit as shown in Figure 10; repeat for four of these units.

Step 9. Measure and mark centers of pieced section. Match center of one pieced border strip to center of pieced section; pin with right sides together. Stitch in place; press seam toward cream/green border strip. Repeat with remaining strips on all

sides of pieced center; press seam toward cream/green border strip. *Note: The strip-pieced border will not reach to the end of all sides.*

Step 10. Place a straight-edge ruler diagonally from corner to corner of the cream/green border to find quilt center. Lay a rotary ruler perpendicular to the straight-edge ruler 1/4"

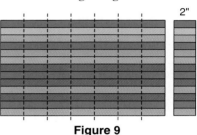

2"

Figure 9
Cut pieced strip into 2" segments.

Figure 10
Join 2 pieced segments on
short ends to make 1 strip.

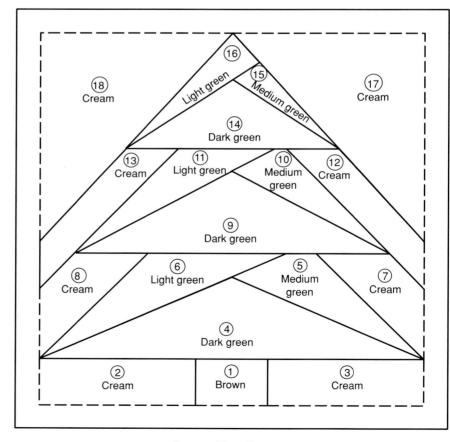

Spruce Tree Coaster
Full-size Pattern

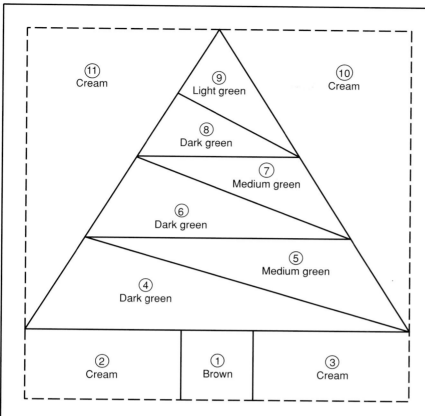

Pine Tree Coaster
Full-size Pattern

Labels within:
⑪ Cream ⑨ Light green ⑩ Cream
⑧ Dark green
⑦ Medium green
⑥ Dark green
⑤ Medium green
④ Dark green
② Cream ① Brown ③ Cream

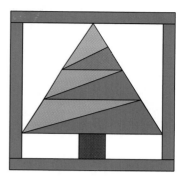

Pine Tree Coaster
Placement Diagram
4 1/2" x 4 1/2"

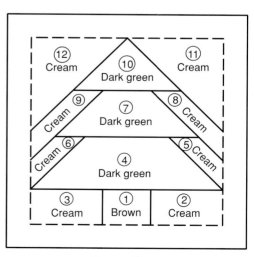

Spruce Tree Coaster
Placement Diagram
4 1/2" x 4 1/2"

Section 1

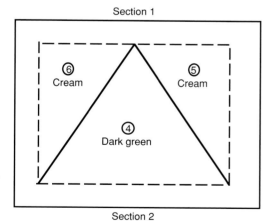

⑥ Cream   ⑤ Cream
④ Dark green

Section 2

② Cream ① Brown ③ Cream

Pine Tree
Full-size Pattern
(2 sections)

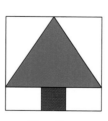

Pine Tree
2" x 2" Block

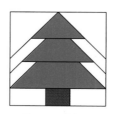

Spruce Tree
2" x 2" Block

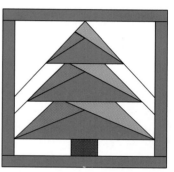

⑫ Cream ⑩ Dark green ⑪ Cream
⑨ Cream ⑦ Dark green ⑧ Cream
⑥ Cream ⑤ Cream
④ Dark green
③ Cream ① Brown ② Cream

Spruce Tree
Full-size Pattern

beyond the corner of the cream/green print border. Cut along this edge as shown in Figure 11; discard cut-off excess.

Step 11. Cut two squares dark green print 4" x 4". Cut each square in half on both diagonals to make quarter-square triangles. Sew a triangle to opposite sides of each 2" tree block referring to Figure 12 to make corner units; press seams toward blocks.

Step 12. Sew a corner unit to each corner of pieced center referring to the Placement Diagram for positioning of block; press seams toward corner units.

Step 13. Cut one piece each dark green print (for backing) and batting 18" x 18".

Step 14. Finish wall quilt as desired referring to General Instructions.

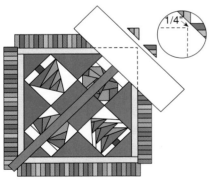

Figure 11
Lay ruler 1/4" from border seam as shown.

Figure 12
Sew a triangle to opposite sides of a tree block to make corner units.

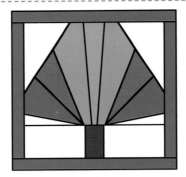

Oak Tree Coaster
Placement Diagram
4 1/2" x 4 1/2"

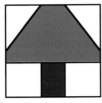

Oak Tree
2" x 2" Block

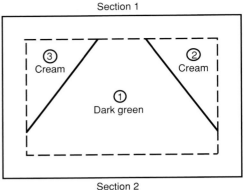

Section 1

③ Cream   ② Cream
① Dark green

Section 2

③ Cream   ① Brown   ② Cream

Oak Tree
Full-size Pattern
(2 sections)

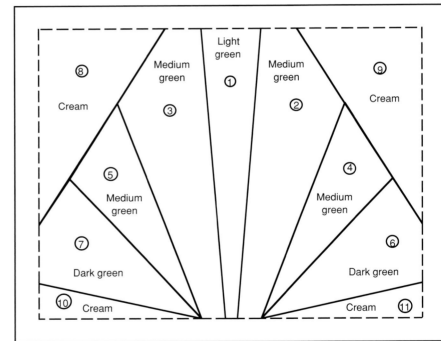

Section 1

⑧ Cream
Medium green
Light green ①
Medium green ②
⑨ Cream
③
⑤ Medium green
④
Medium green
⑦
Dark green
⑥
Dark green
⑩ Cream
⑪ Cream

Section 2

③ cream   ① brown   ② cream

Oak Tree Coaster
Full-size pattern in 2 sections

Section 2

⑤

④

③

Assorted greens

②

①

Section 1

⑤ Cream

①

Assorted greens

②

③

④ Cream

④

③

Assorted greens

②

⑤ Cream

①

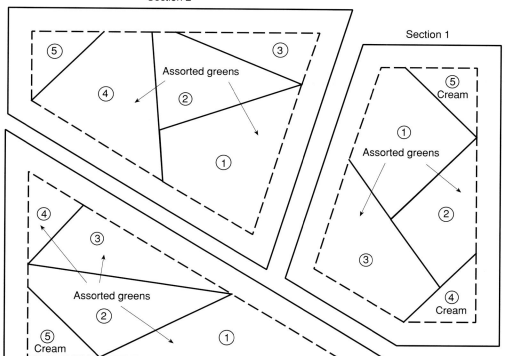

Section 3
Section 4

③ Cream

① Brown

② Cream

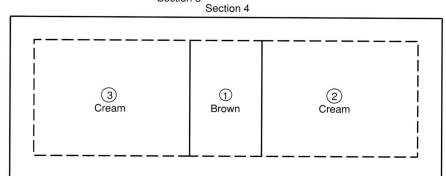

Maple Tree Coaster
Full-size pattern in 4 sections

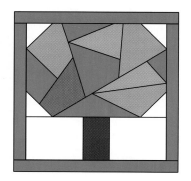

Maple Tree Coaster
Placement Diagram
4 1/2" x 4 1/2"

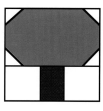

Maple Tree
2" x 2" Block

Section 1

⑤

Cream

②

1
Dark green

④

Cream

③

Section 2

③ Cream

① Brown

② Cream

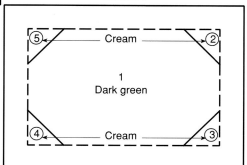

Maple Tree
Full-size Pattern
(2 sections)

Welcome Wreath

By Norma Storm

Stitch this cheerful, pretty and surprisingly easy-to-make wall quilt or miniature to welcome spring.

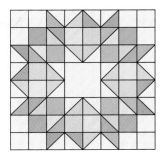

Welcome Wreath
16" x 16" Block

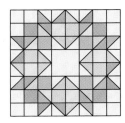

Welcome Wreath Miniature
10" x 10" Block

Specifications

Skill Level: Beginner

Wall Quilt Size: 24" x 24"

Block Size: 16" x 16"

Number of Blocks: 1

Materials

3/4 yard cream-on-cream print

Scraps blue, lavender, pink, green, yellow and peach pastel prints or solids for piecing

Scraps rose-colored solid or prints for flowers

Scraps green print for leaves and stems

Backing 28" x 28"

Batting 28" x 28"

All-purpose thread to match fabrics

1 spool off-white quilting thread

2 3/4 yards self-made or purchased binding

Basic sewing tools and supplies

Welcome Wreath

Instructions

Step 1. Cut the following 2 7/8" x 2 7/8" squares from scrap fabrics in suggested colors: blues—4; lavenders—2; pinks—6; greens—4; yellows—2; peach—2; and cream-on-cream print—12. Cut each square in half on one diagonal to make triangles.

Step 2. Cut one square cream-on-cream print 4 1/2" x 4 1/2". Cut four squares each green, yellow, blue and pink and 12 squares cream 2 1/2" x 2 1/2".

Step 3. Arrange the squares and triangles in rows referring to Figure 1. Join the triangles in each row to make triangle/squares before joining with squares to make rows. Join rows to complete pieced center.

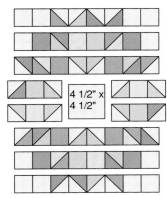

4 1/2" x 4 1/2"

Figure 1
Arrange squares and triangles in rows as shown.

Step 4. Cut two strips cream-on-cream print 4 1/2" x 16 1/2"; sew to opposite sides of pieced center referring to Figure 2. Cut two more strips cream-on-cream print 4 1/2" x

24 1/2"; sew to top and bottom. Press seams toward strips.

Step 5. Prepare templates for flower, leaf and stem pieces using full-size pattern motif given. Cut each shape as directed on pieces, adding a seam allowance when cutting for hand-appliqué.

Step 6. Hand-appliqué a flower, leaf and stem motif to each corner on border strips in numerical order, over-

4 1/2" x 24 1/2"

4 1/2" x 16 1/2"

Figure 2
Add border strips to pieced center as shown.

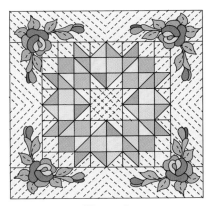

Figure 3
Draw quilting lines 3/4" apart on the diagonal as shown.

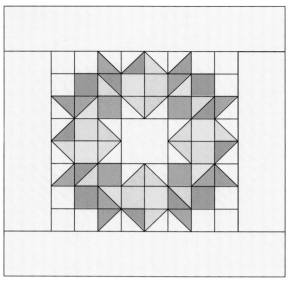

Welcome Wreath Miniature
Placement Diagram
14 1/2" x 14 1/2"

Welcome Wreath
Placement Diagram
24" x 24"

lapping pieces using full-size drawing as a guide for placement of pieces.

Step 7. Mark background quilting design with diagonal lines spaced 3/4" apart referring to project photo and Figure 3 for positioning.

Step 8. Finish referring to General Instructions.

Welcome Wreath Miniature

Specifications
Skill Level: Beginner
Miniature Size: 14 1/2" x 14 1/2"
Block Size: 10" x 10"
Number of Blocks: 1

Materials
1/2 yard cream-on-cream print
Scraps blue, lavender, pink, green, yellow and peach pastel prints or solids for piecing
Backing 17" x 17"
Batting 17" x 17"
Neutral color all-purpose thread
1 spool off-white quilting thread
2 yards self-made or purchased binding
Basic sewing tools and supplies

Instructions

Step 1. Cut the following 2 1/8" x 2 1/8" squares: pink—6; lavender—2; yellow—2; green—4; blue—4; and cream-on-cream print—12. Cut each square in half on one diagonal to make triangles.

Step 2. Cut four 1 3/4" x 1 3/4" squares from each of the following colors: blue, green, pink and yellow. Cut 12 squares cream-on-cream print 1 3/4" x 1 3/4" and one sqare 3" x 3".

Step 3. Lay out squares with triangles in rows referring to Figure 4. Join the triangles in each row to make triangle/squares before joining with squares to make rows. Join rows to complete pieced center.

Step 4. Cut two strips cream-on-cream print 2 3/4" x 10 1/2"; sew to opposite sides of pieced center referring to Figure 5. Cut two trips cream-on-cream print 2 3/4" x 15"; sew to top and bottom. Press seams toward strips.

Step 5. Finish as for Wall Quilt.

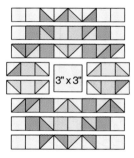

Figure 4
Arrange squares and triangles in rows as shown.

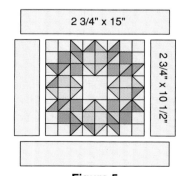

Figure 5
Add border strips to pieced center as shown.

Rose, Leaf & Stem Appliqué Pattern
Cut pieces as directed in each piece for color. Cut each piece, adding a seam allowance when cutting. Appliqué pieces in numerical order, overlapping pieces as indicated on pattern.

Summer Festivities

Summer is full of patriotic holidays, vacations, gardening, days at the lake and those hot and humid dog days of August. Create your own fireworks this summer with a dazzling wall quilt or stitch a special birthday quilt to use for all your birthday celebrations. You'll find wall quilts to help you enjoy all those lazy days of summer.

Stitch this bright and cheerful quilt using fusible appliqué for the dog and sun and colorful fabric scraps for the borders. It won't take long to make, and you'll still have plenty of time to enjoy the celebrations, parties and outdoor activities of the summer months.
Dog Days of Summer pattern begins on page 92.

Sun Half-Block
10" x 21" Block
Make 4

Sun
15" x 15" Block
Make 1

Dog
10" x 10" Block

Dog Days of Summer

By Ann Boyce

Dog days—those hot and humid days in August when it seems like there is no relief in sight. In the middle of winter when you can't stand the cold, this quilt will cheer you up with its bright colors and reminders of the dog days of summer.

Specifications

Skill Level: Beginner

Wall Quilt Size: 47" x 47"

Block Size: 3" x 3", 10" x 10", 10" x 21" and 15" x 15"

Number of Blocks: 4 Four-Patch blocks, 4 Dog blocks, 4 Half-Sun blocks and 1 Sun block

Materials

1/4 yard each turquoise, purple, yellow, lime green, hot pink, orange, blue dots and blue star prints

1/2 yard black solid

1/2 yard white solid

1 yard yellow solid or tie-dyed fabric

1 1/4 yards blue print

Backing 51" x 51"

Batting 51" x 51"

5 1/2 yards self-made or purchased binding

1 spool each yellow, black and white all-purpose thread

1 1/2 yards fusible transfer web

1 1/2 yards tear-off fabric stabilizer

8 (1") yellow buttons

4 large black ball buttons

Basic sewing supplies and tools

Instructions

Step 1. Cut four squares yellow solid 10 1/2" x 10 1/2".

Step 2. Iron fusible web to wrong side of remaining yellow fabric. Trace two 12" circles on the paper side of fusible web for half-sun. Cut each circle in half. Trace one 5 1/4" circle on the paper side of fusible web for sun. Trace both sizes of rays using patterns given. Cut out shapes; remove paper backing.

Step 3. Cut two strips blue print 10 1/2" by fabric width. Cut into four rectangles 10 1/2" x 21 1/2". Cut one square 15 1/2" x 15 1/2" blue print; fold and crease to mark center.

Step 4. Fold and mark center of 5 1/4" circle. Place circle in center of 15 1/2" blue print square and arrange nine small sun rays around and under edge of circle, overlapping as necessary referring to Figure 1. Fuse pieces in place.

Figure 1
Arrange small rays around sun piece.

Step 5. Fold and crease 10 1/2" x 21 1/2" rectangles to find center. Fold half-sun pieces to find center; center on rectangles. Arrange seven large sun rays around and under half-sun pieces, overlapping as necessary referring to Figure 2. Fuse in place.

Figure 2
Arrange large rays around half-sun piece.

Step 6. Place stabilizer behind each design. Using yellow thread, machine-appliqué shapes in place on blocks, starting with rays and ending with sun shapes.

Dog Days of Summer
Placement Diagram
47" x 47"

Figure 3
Arrange blocks as shown.

Figure 4
Make a Four-Patch
block as shown.

Step 7. Cut six squares from each bright print 3 7/8" x 3 7/8". Cut each square in half on one diagonal to make triangles. Join different colored triangles to make squares; repeat for 24 pieced squares. Join five squares to make a strip; repeat for two strips. Sew a strip to opposite sides of the appliquéd center. Press seams toward center. Join seven squares to make a strip; repeat for two strips. Sew a strip to remaining sides of appliquéd center; press seams toward center.

Step 8. Fuse transfer web to wrong side of black and white solids. Trace dog heads onto paper side of black solid and dog faces onto paper side of white solid. Cut out shapes.

Step 9. Arrange a dog head and face on each 10 1/2" x 10 1/2" yellow square referring to the Placement

Diagram for positioning; fuse in place. Machine-appliqué in place using black thread on dogs' heads and white thread on faces.

Step 10. Arrange blocks as shown in Figure 3. Join in rows; join rows to complete center; press.

Step 11. Cut one strip from each of the eight bright prints 2 1/2" by fabric width. Sew strips together in groups of four to make two pieced sections; press seams in one direction. Cut pieced sections into 3 1/2" segments.

Step 12. Join five segments on short sides to make a strip; repeat for four strips. Sew a strip to opposite sides of the pieced center. *Note: Mathematically, these strips are 1" short of the quilt's edge measurements. Adjust seams when joining strips to allow for fitting.* Press seams toward strips.

Step 13. Cut eight each black and white solid squares 2" x 2". Sew a black square to a white square; repeat for eight units. Join two units to make a Four-Patch block as shown in Figure 4; repeat for four blocks.

Step 14. Sew a Four-Patch block to each end of the remaining two pieced strips. Sew a strip to remaining sides of pieced center. Press seams toward strips.

Step 15. Prepare quilt top for quilting and finish as in General Instructions.

Step 16. Sew one black and two yellow buttons on each dog face as marked on patterns for positioning to finish.

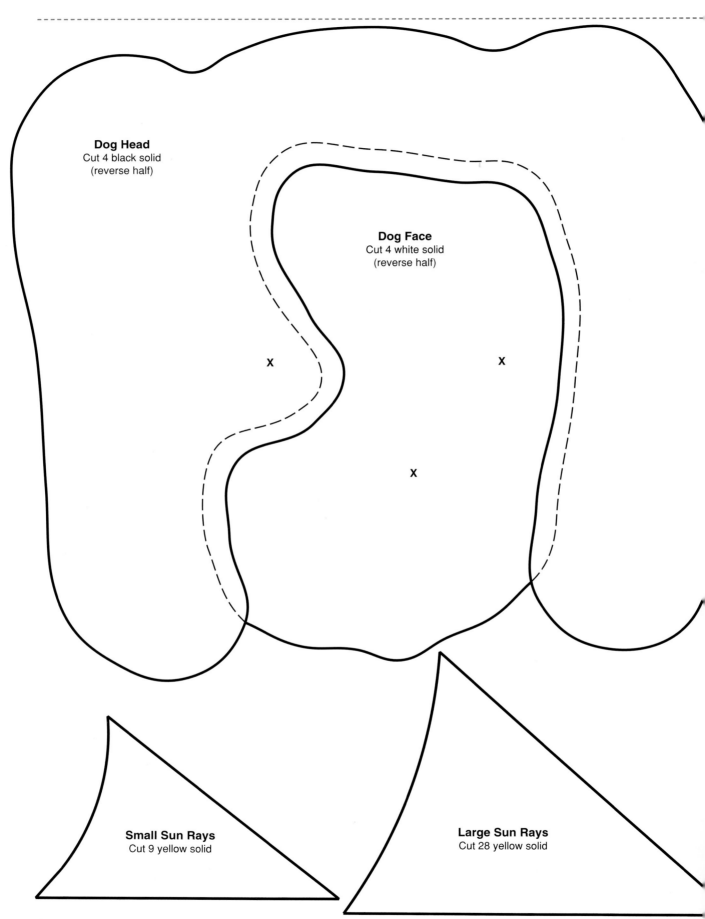

Dog Head
Cut 4 black solid
(reverse half)

Dog Face
Cut 4 white solid
(reverse half)

X

X

X

Small Sun Rays
Cut 9 yellow solid

Large Sun Rays
Cut 28 yellow solid

Home in the Garden

By Christine Schultz

This small wall quilt features simple piecing and appliqué. It's a perfect showcase for scraps of favorite fabrics and old buttons.

2" x 10 1/2"

1/2" x 6 1/2"

2" x 17"

1/2" x 16"

Home in the Garden
Placement Diagram
10 1/2" x 21"

Specifications

Skill Level: Intermediate

Wall Quilt Size: 10 1/2" x 21"

Materials

1/8 yard each red check and background

1/4 yard each blue and green prints

1/3 yard border fabric

1 fat quarter dark brown print

Scraps for flowers and entrance

Backing 13" x 24"

Batting 13" x 24"

2 yards self-made or purchased binding

All-purpose thread to match fabrics

1 spool white quilting thread

Tracing paper

Freezer paper

4 buttons of different sizes and colors

Basic sewing supplies and tools and tweezers

Instructions

Step 1. Cut one strip each 1 1/2" x 18" blue print and red check. Join strips along length. Cut apart to make two 1 1/2" x 9" segments. Join these segments along length to make a pieced strip as shown in Figure 1.

Step 2. Cut strip apart in 1 1/2" segments. Join five segments as

Figure 1
Join strip sets as shown.

Figure 2
Join 5 segments as shown.

Figure 3
Sew A to 1 short side of pieced birdhouse base.

shown in Figure 2 to make the birdhouse base.

Step 3. Cut an A triangle from red check. Sew the triangle to one short end of the birdhouse base as shown in Figure 3.

Step 4. Cut two strips background fabric 1 1/4" x 6". Sew one of these strips to two opposite sides of the birdhouse base; place a straight-edge ruler on the edge of the top triangle and trim strips at the same angle as shown in Figure 4.

Figure 4
Trim strips even with edge of A.

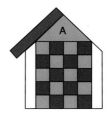

Figure 5
Sew a strip to left side of A.

Step 5. Cut two strips brown print 1 1/4" x 6". Sew a strip to the left side of A as shown in Figure 5; press seam toward strip. Repeat for right

side. Trim strips even with side piece as shown in Figure 6.

Step 6. Cut two A triangles from background fabric. Sew a triangle to each side of the birdhouse section to

Figure 6
Trim even with side strips.

Figure 7
Sew A triangles to top
of pieced section.

complete as shown in Figure 7. Cut hole piece; appliqué in the center of birdhouse referring to the Placement Diagram and photo of project for positioning.

Step 7. Cut one strip brown print 1 1/2" x 8 1/2". Cut two strips background 2 3/4" x 8 1/2". Sew the brown strip between the two background strips.

Step 8. Sew the brown/background section to the bottom of the birdhouse section.

Step 9. Cut two strips blue print 1" x 16 1/2"; sew a strip to opposite long

sides of the pieced center. Press seams toward strips.

Step 10. Cut two strips blue print 1" x 7"; sew a strip to top and bottom of the pieced center. Press seams toward strips.

Step 11. Cut two strips border fabric 2 1/2" x 17 1/2"; sew a strip to opposite long sides of the pieced center. Press seams toward strips.

Step 12. Cut two strips border fabric 2 1/2" x 11"; sew a strip to top and bottom of pieced center. Press seams toward strips.

Step 13. Draw a full-size pattern for appliqué onto tracing paper. Transfer pattern to bottom half of pieced center using a water-erasable marker or pencil.

Step 14. Cut 1/2"-wide bias strip from green print to make an 18" piece. Press or baste in edges 1/8". Appliqué in place using drawing as a guide for placement of stems.

Step 15. Cut finished-size pieces for each pattern shape from freezer paper. Iron freezer-paper shapes to the wrong side of the flower and leaf scraps as directed on each piece for color.

Step 16. Cut out shapes leaving 3/16" turn-under allowance around each piece. Pin the pieces in place on background using traced lines as guides for placement.

Step 17. Using matching thread and a needle to help turn edges over paper shapes,

appliqué pieces in place, layering as necessary to complete the design.

Step 18. When appliqué is complete, carefully slit behind pieces from the backside; remove freezer paper using tweezers, if necessary. Press piece from right side.

Step 19. Prepare for quilting and finish referring to General Instructions.

Step 20. Sew a button in the center of each flower after binding and quilting are complete.

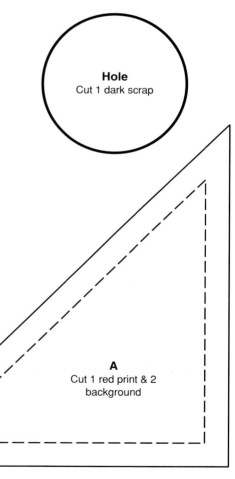

Hole
Cut 1 dark scrap

A
Cut 1 red print & 2
background

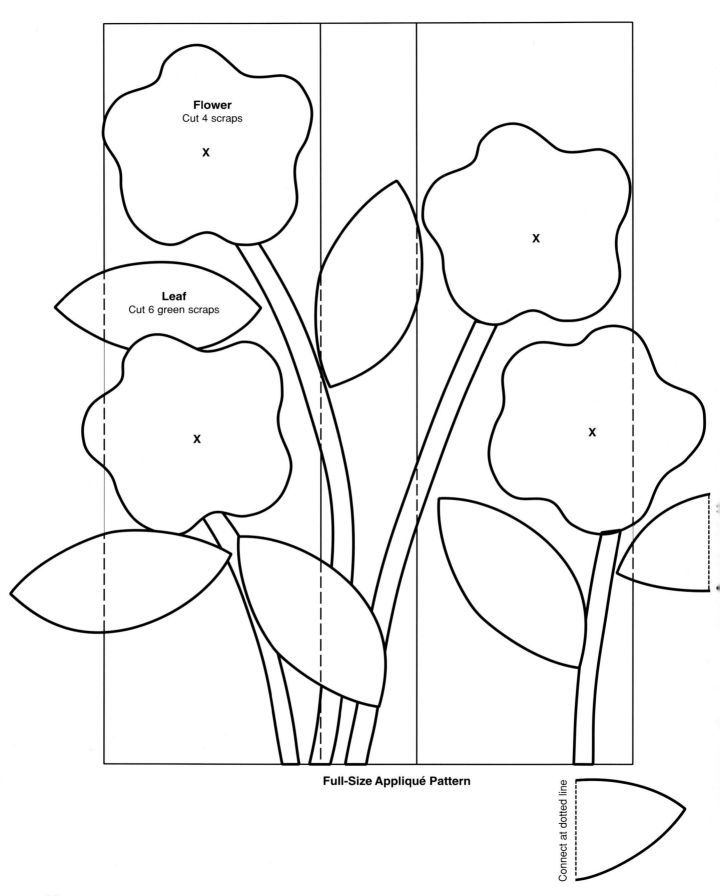

Flower
Cut 4 scraps

X

Leaf
Cut 6 green scraps

X

X

X

Full-Size Appliqué Pattern

Connect at dotted line

Stars & Stripes

By Ann Boyce

Red, white and blue combine with buttons to make this attractive wall quilt. Proudly display it for the Fourth of July or patriotic holidays throughout the year.

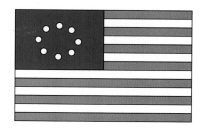

Stars & Stripes
13" x 20" Block

Specifications

Skill Level: Beginner

Wall Quilt Size: 47 1/2" x 47 1/2"

Block Size: 13" x 20"

Number of Blocks: 4

Materials

1/2 yard dark blue solid

3/4 yard each medium blue star and white-on-white prints

1 1/4 yards red print

Backing 52" x 52"

Batting 52" x 52"

6 yards self-made or purchased binding

52 (1/2") white buttons

All-purpose thread to match fabrics

1 spool clear nylon monofilament

Basic sewing supplies and tools

Instructions

Step 1. Cut the following strips across the width of the fabrics: red print—11 strips 1 1/2" wide; white-on-white print—nine strips 1 1/2" wide; blue solid—one strip 7 1/2" wide; and blue star print—six strips 2" wide.

Stars & Stripes
Placement Diagram
47 1/2" x 47 1/2"

Step 2. Join three red and three white print strips beginning with white and ending with red as shown in Figure 1; repeat for a second strip set. Press seams in one direction.

Step 3. Cut each strip set apart in 20 1/2" rectangles for Unit 1; you will need four Unit 1 rectangles.

Step 4. Join four red and three white print strips beginning and ending with a red strip as shown in Figure 2; press seams in one direction. Cut

Figure 1
Join strips as shown. Cut in 20 1/2" segments for Unit 1.

20 1/2"   *20 1/2"*

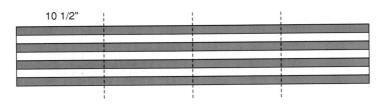

Figure 2
Join strips as shown. Cut in 10 1/2" segments for Unit 2.

strip set apart in 10 1/2" rectangles for Unit 2; you will need four Unit 2 rectangles.

Step 5. Cut four 7 1/2" x 10 1/2" segments from the 7 1/2"-wide blue solid strip.

Step 6. Join Unit 2 and a 7 1/2" x 10 1/2" blue solid rectangle with Unit 1 to complete one block as shown in Figure 3; press. Repeat for four blocks.

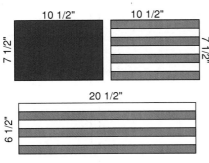

Figure 3
Join units as shown to complete block.

Step 7. Cut eight strips 2" x 13 1/2" from 2"-wide blue star print. Sew a strip to each short side of the pieced blocks; press seams toward strips.

Step 8. Cut one square blue star print 9" x 9". Arrange pieced blocks with this square as shown in Figure 4. Join pieces, again referring to Figure 4. Press.

Figure 4
Arrange pieced blocks around center square; join as shown.

Step 9. Cut two strips blue star print 2" x 35". Sew a strip to top and bottom of the pieced section; press seams toward strips. Cut two strips blue star print 2" x 38". Sew a strip to remaining sides of the pieced section; press seams toward strips.

Step 10. Cut eight strips white print and 12 strips red print 1 1/2" by fabric width. Sew strips together in four sets of five, beginning and ending with red print strips. Press seams in one direction. Repeat for four strip sets for borders. Cut each set into 38"-long strips.

Step 11. Sew a strip to two opposite sides of the pieced section.

Step 12. Cut four squares blue solid 5 1/2" x 5 1/2". Sew a square to each end of the pieced border strips. Sew one of these strips to each remaining side; press seams toward strips.

Step 13. Prepare quilt top for quilting and finish as in General Instructions. *Note: The quilt shown was machine-quilted using clear monofilament in the top of the machine and all-purpose thread in the bobbin.*

Step 14. Sew eight buttons on each blue section of each block and five buttons on each border corner block referring to the Placement Diagram and photo for positioning.

Born on the Fourth of July

By Jill Reber

Use patriotic fabrics to create this star design in honor of Independence Day. The quilt shown could be used on the wall or on a table. Show your patriotic spirit by displaying this quick and easy project.

Twirling Star
8" x 8" Block

Specifications

Skill Level: Beginner

Wall Quilt Size: 40" x 40"

Block Size: 8" x 8"

Number of Blocks: 9

Materials

5/8 yard flag print

1/2 yard each light beige, navy, red/tan and red prints

Backing 44" x 44"

Batting 44" x 44"

4 3/4 yards self-made or purchased binding

All-purpose thread to match fabrics

Basic sewing supplies and tools, rotary cutter, ruler and cutting mat

Instructions

Step 1. Cut one strip 2 7/8" by fabric width and two strips 5 1/4" by fabric width red print. Cut 2 7/8" strips into 2 7/8" segments; cut each seg-

5 1/4"

5 1/4"

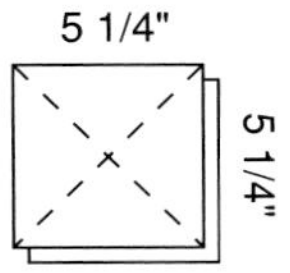

Figure 1
Cut squares in half on both diagonals to make A triangles.

ment in half on one diagonal to make 36 B triangles. Cut 5 1/4" strips into 5 1/4" segments; cut each segment in half on both diagonals as shown in Figure 1 for 36 A triangles.

Step 2. Cut two strips 5 1/4" by fabric width and one strip 3 3/8" by fabric width light beige. Cut 5 1/4" strips into 5 1/4" segments; cut each segment in half on both diagonals for 36 A triangles. Cut each 3 3/8" strip into 3 3/8" segments for 9 C squares.

Step 3. Cut two strips 5 1/4" by fabric width navy print. Cut each strip into 5 1/4" segments. Cut each segment twice on the diagonal to make 36 A triangles.

Step 4. Sew a beige A to navy print A to make a square as shown in Figure 2; repeat for 36 units.

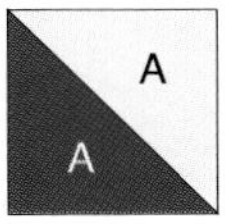

A

A

Figure 2
Join A triangles to make squares; repeat for 36 units.

Step 5. Sew red print A triangles to opposite sides of A-A units as shown in Figure 3; repeat for 18 units.

Step 6. Sew an A-A unit to opposite sides of C as shown in Figure 4; repeat for nine units.

Figure 3
Sew a red print A to opposite sides of A-A squares; repeat for 18 units.

Figure 4
Sew A-A units to opposite sides of C; repeat for 9 units.

Step 7. Join pieced units and B as shown in Figure 5 to complete one block; repeat for nine blocks.

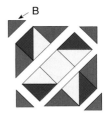

Figure 5
Join units to complete 1 block; repeat for 9 blocks.

Step 8. Cut two strips 8 1/2" by fabric width red/tan print. Cut strips into 2 1/2" segments. You will need 24 segments for sashing strips.

Step 9. Cut one strip navy print 2 1/2" by fabric width. Cut into 2 1/2" segments. You will need 16 segments for sashing squares.

Step 10. Join four sashing strips with three Twirling Star blocks to make a block row as shown in Figure 6. Repeat for three rows; press.

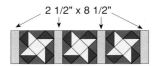

2 1/2" x 8 1/2"

Figure 6
Make a block row as shown.

Step 11. Join four sashing squares with three sashing strips to make a sashing row as shown in Figure 7. Repeat for four rows; press.

Step 12. Join sashing rows with block rows, beginning and ending with a sashing row; press.

Step 13. Cut two strips flag print 4 1/2" x 32 1/2"; sew to top and bottom of pieced center. Press seams toward strips. Cut two strips flag print 4 1/2" x 40 1/2"; sew to opposite sides of pieced center. Press seams toward strips.

Step 14. Prepare quilt for quilting and finish referring to General Instructions.

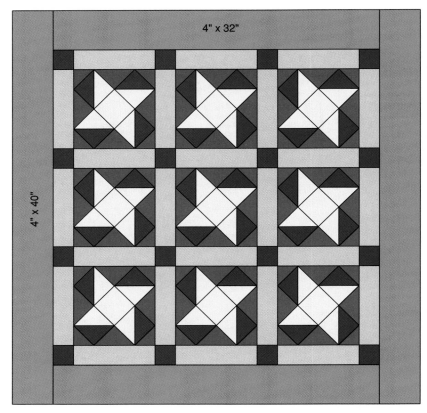

4" x 32"

4" x 40"

Born on the Fourth of July
Placement Diagram
40" x 40"

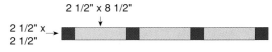

2 1/2" x 8 1/2"

2 1/2" x
2 1/2"

Figure 7
Make a sashing row as shown.

Fireworks

By Norma Storm

Fireworks light up the night sky with bright colors. Bring them inside with this dazzling quilt using a mixture of fabrics, colors and textures to reflect their breathtaking beauty.

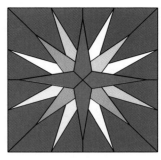

Mariner's Compass
27" x 27" Block

Specifications

Skill Level: Experienced

Quilt Size: 73 1/2" x 73 1/2"

Block Size: 27" x 27"

Number of Blocks: 1 quarter block, 4 half-blocks and 4 whole blocks

Materials

1/4–1/2 yard each light and medium yellow; light, medium and dark pink; light and medium orange; white; lights, medium and dark blue; red and dark red; aqua solids

4 1/2 yards navy blue solid

Backing 78" x 78"

Batting 78" x 78"

9 yards self-made or purchased binding

Basic sewing supplies and tools

Project Note

Purchase a variety of solid-color fabrics in different textures and finishes. The list of materials includes a range from 1/4 to 1/2 yard of each color. The amount depends on how you chose to place your colors. The quilt shown has a rather random color arrangement. The drawings and templates reflect the number to cut to duplicate the quilt exactly, but you may choose to change the colors. If you purchase 1/2 yard of each fabric, you may need to use only four or five fabrics to create your quilt. Because the pieces are large, it

Fireworks
Placement Diagram
73 1/2" x 73 1/2"

would be difficult to cut many pieces from a 1/4-yard piece; fat quarters would work better.

Be creative and place the colors as you like to create an interesting and colorful quilt similar to, but not exactly like the one shown.

Instructions

Step 1. Prepare templates using pat-

Color Key
- ■ Dark red
- ■ Red
- ■ Dark pink
- ☐ Medium pink
- ☐ Light pink
- ☐ Medium yellow
- ☐ Light yellow
- ■ Medium orange
- ☐ Light orange
- ■ Dark blue
- ■ Medium blue
- ☐ Light blue
- ■ Navy blue
- ■ Aqua
- ☐ White

tern pieces given. Cut as directed on each piece.

Step 2. Sew D and E to C as shown in Figure 1; repeat for four units. Sew ER and DR to C as shown in Figure 1; repeat for four units.

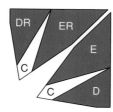

Figure 1
Sew D and E to C. Sew
ER and DR to C.

Step 3. Join the two D-E-C units with B as shown in Figure 2; repeat for remaining units.

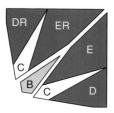

Figure 2
Join the 2 pieced units with B.

Step 4. Join two B-D-E-C units with A as shown in Figure 3; repeat for remaining units.

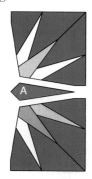

Figure 3
Join 2 pieced units with A.

Step 5. Join the two pieced units with two A pieces to complete one whole block as shown in Figure 4; repeat for four blocks.

Step 6. Join pieces as shown in

Figure 5 to make half-blocks; repeat for four half-blocks.

Make 4

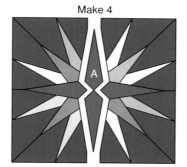

Figure 4
Join 2 units with 2 A pieces
to complete block.

Make 4

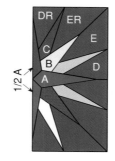

Figure 5
Make a half-block as shown.

Step 7. Join pieces as shown in Figure 6 to make a quarter-block.

Make 1

Figure 6
Make a quarter-block as shown.

Step 8. Cut four strips navy blue solid 3 1/2" x 27 1/2". Join two whole blocks and one half block with two strips as shown in Figure 7. Join one whole block and one half block as shown in Figure 8; repeat.

Step 9. Cut one strip navy blue solid 3 1/2" x 14". Join one half-block and one quarter-block with the strip as shown in Figure 9.

Figure 7
Join units as shown.

Figure 8
Join units as shown.

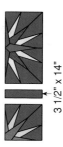

Figure 9
Join units as shown.

Step 10. Cut two strips navy blue solid 3 1/2" x 44". Using one strip, join one half-block/whole-block unit with one half-block/quarter-block unit. Sew the remaining 3 1/2" x 44" strip to the bottom of this unit and add a whole block/half-block unit to the bottom of the strip as shown in Figure 10.

Step 11. Cut one strip navy blue solid 3 1/2" x 74"; join the two remaining pieced units with the strip referring to the Placement Diagram to complete piecing.

Step 12. Mark the top with quilting designs given referring to Figure 11 for placement suggestions.

Step 13. Prepare quilt top for quilting referring to General Instructions.

Step 14. Hand-quilt on marked lines using white quilting thread.

Step 15. When quilting is complete, finish referring to General Instructions.

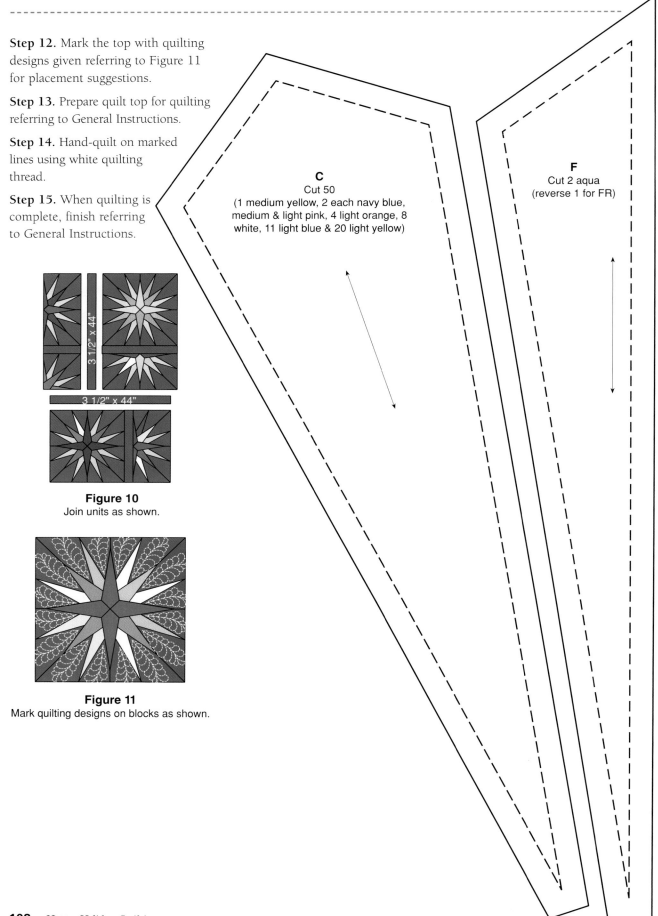

Figure 10
Join units as shown.

3 1/2" x 44"

3 1/2" x 44"

Figure 11
Mark quilting designs on blocks as shown.

C
Cut 50
(1 medium yellow, 2 each navy blue, medium & light pink, 4 light orange, 8 white, 11 light blue & 20 light yellow)

F
Cut 2 aqua
(reverse 1 for FR)

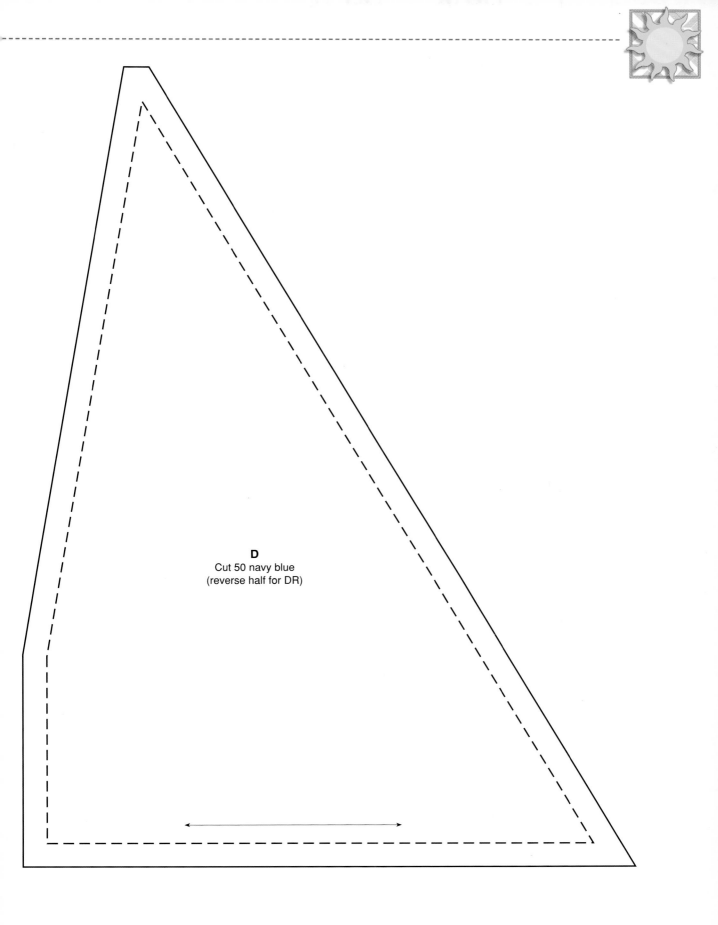

D
Cut 50 navy blue
(reverse half for DR)

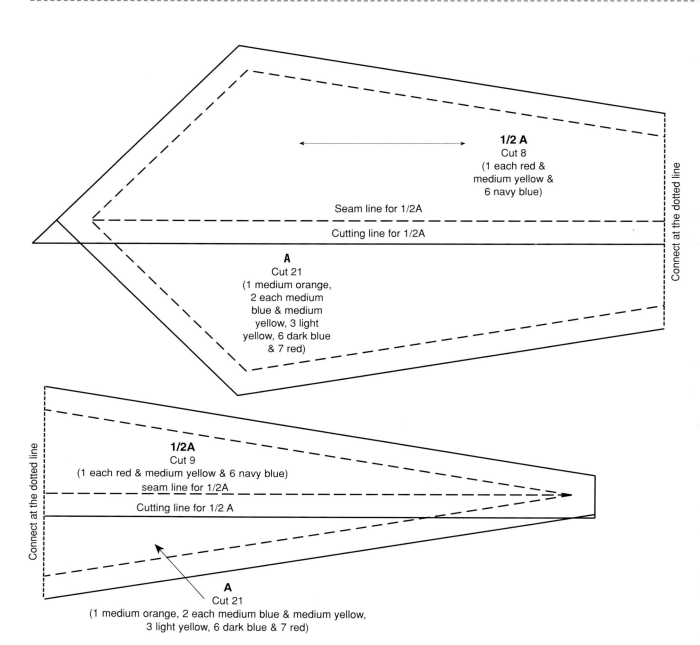

1/2 A
Cut 8
(1 each red &
medium yellow &
6 navy blue)

Seam line for 1/2A

Cutting line for 1/2A

Connect at the dotted line

A
Cut 21
(1 medium orange,
2 each medium
blue & medium
yellow, 3 light
yellow, 6 dark blue
& 7 red)

Connect at the dotted line

1/2A
Cut 9
(1 each red & medium yellow & 6 navy blue)

seam line for 1/2A

Cutting line for 1/2 A

A
Cut 21
(1 medium orange, 2 each medium blue & medium yellow,
3 light yellow, 6 dark blue & 7 red)

Quilting Designs

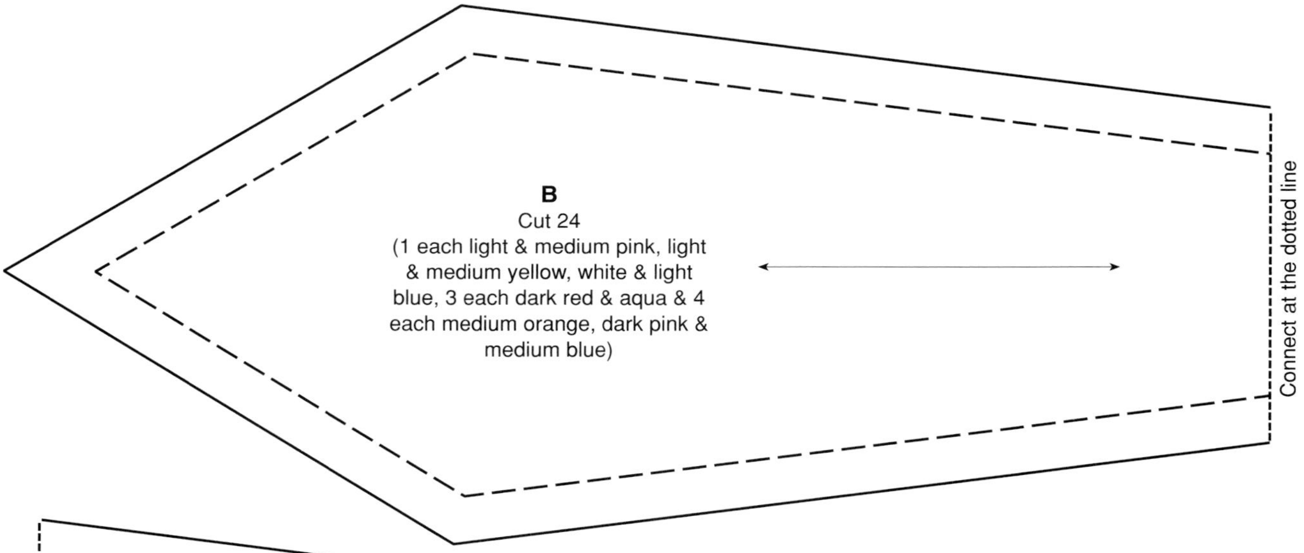

B
Cut 24
(1 each light & medium pink, light
& medium yellow, white & light
blue, 3 each dark red & aqua & 4
each medium orange, dark pink &
medium blue)

Connect at the dotted line

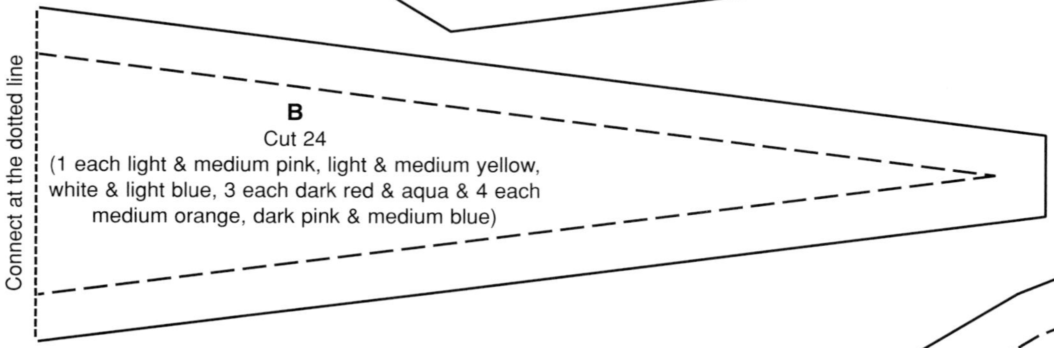

B
Cut 24
(1 each light & medium pink, light & medium yellow,
white & light blue, 3 each dark red & aqua & 4 each
medium orange, dark pink & medium blue)

Connect at the dotted line

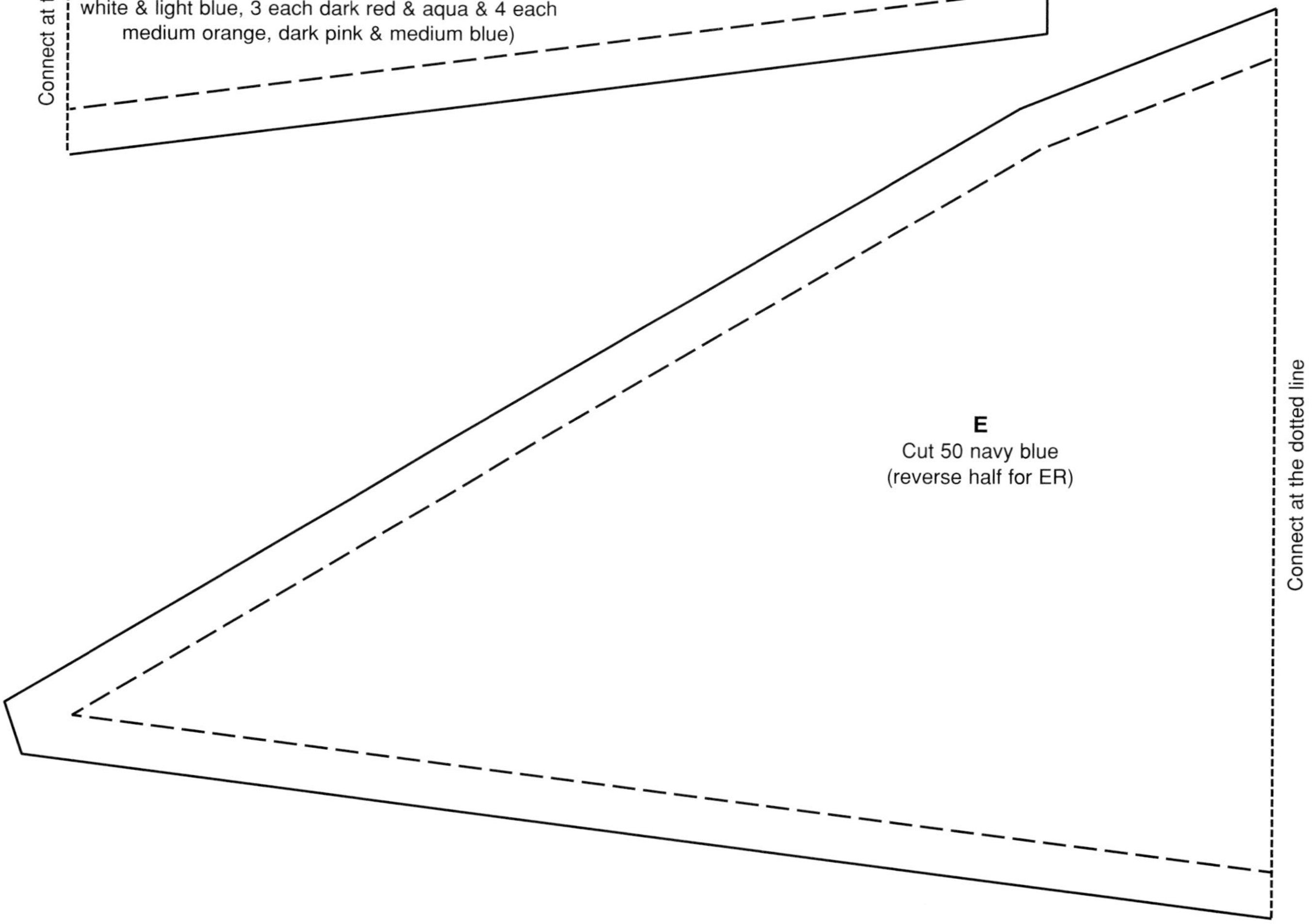

E
Cut 50 navy blue
(reverse half for ER)

Connect at the dotted line

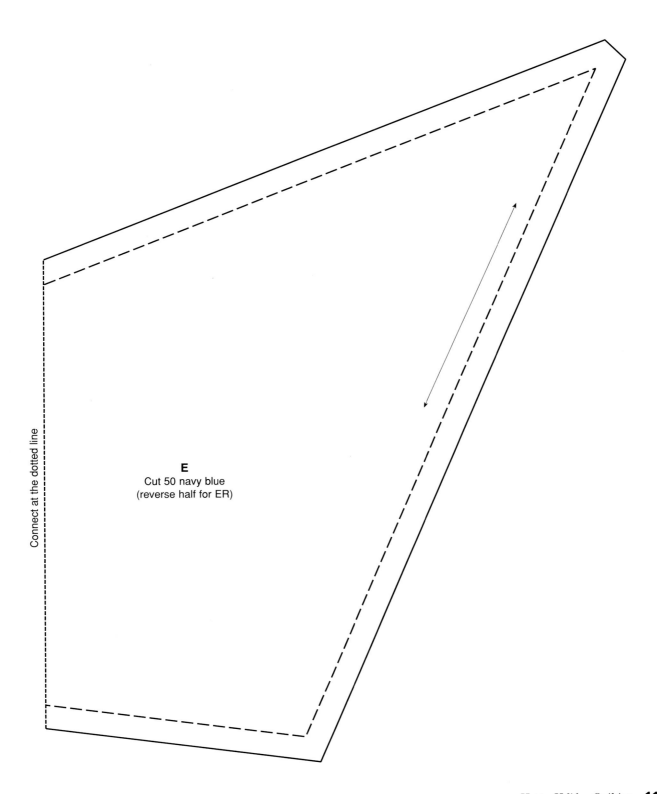

Connect at the dotted line

E
Cut 50 navy blue
(reverse half for ER)

Summer Sailing

By Charlyne Stewart

Celebrate this summer by going sailing. This wall quilt looks as if there are rough seas ahead. If you prefer smooth sailing, use lighter fabrics and smooth out the line of the waves.

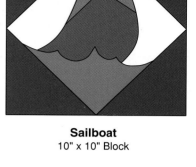

Sailboat
10" x 10" Block

Specifications

Skill Level: Intermediate

Wall Quilt Size: 36" x 36"

Block Size: 10" x 10"

Number of Blocks: 4

Materials

1/8 yard red check

1/4 yard each white and royal blue solids and light blue pin dot

1/2 yard each red solid, dark blue moiré, dark blue print and light blue print

Backing 40" x 40"

Batting 40" x 40"

1 spool each red, light and dark blue all-purpose thread

1 spool silver metallic thread

1 spool blue quilting thread

1/2 yard fusible transfer web

Instructions

Step 1. Prepare templates for pieces A–E using pattern pieces given. Cut as directed on each piece.

Step 2. On the smooth side of the fusible webbing, mark four each sailboats, chevrons and water shapes. Cut pieces leaving space around each piece; fuse to the wrong side of designated fabrics following manufacturer's instructions.

Step 3. Cut out shapes on traced lines; remove paper backing.

Step 4. Cut four squares white solid 7 1/2" x 7 1/2". Sew an E triangle to each side of each square; press seams toward E.

Step 5. Position sailboat, chevron and water on white square referring to Placement Diagram and photo. Fuse shapes in place following manufacturer's instructions; repeat for four blocks.

Step 6. Machine-appliqué pieces in place with a slightly open, medium width zigzag stitch, using matching thread. Trim loose threads. Repeat for four blocks; set aside.

Step 7. Sew B and BR to A as shown in Figure 1; repeat for 12 units. Sew D to each side of C as shown in Figure 2; repeat for nine units.

Step 8. Join three C-D units with two A-B units to make a sashing row as shown in Figure 3; repeat for three rows.

Step 9. Join two appliquéd blocks with three A-B units to make a block row; repeat for two rows. Join the block rows with the sashing rows to complete the center.

Step 10. Cut two strips red solid 2 1/2" x 32 1/2"; sew a strip to opposite sides. Cut two more strips red solid 2 1/2" x 36 1/2"; sew to top and bottom. Press seams toward strips.

Step 11. Prepare top for quilting and finishing referring to General Instructions. *Note: The quilt shown was machine-quilted using silver metallic thread in the top of the machine and all-purpose thread to match backing in the bobbin. It was hand-quilted in the ditch of seams with blue quilting thread.*

Figure 1
Sew B and BR pieces to A.

Figure 2
Sew D to C.

Figure 3
Join 3 C-D units with 2 A-B units to make a sashing row.

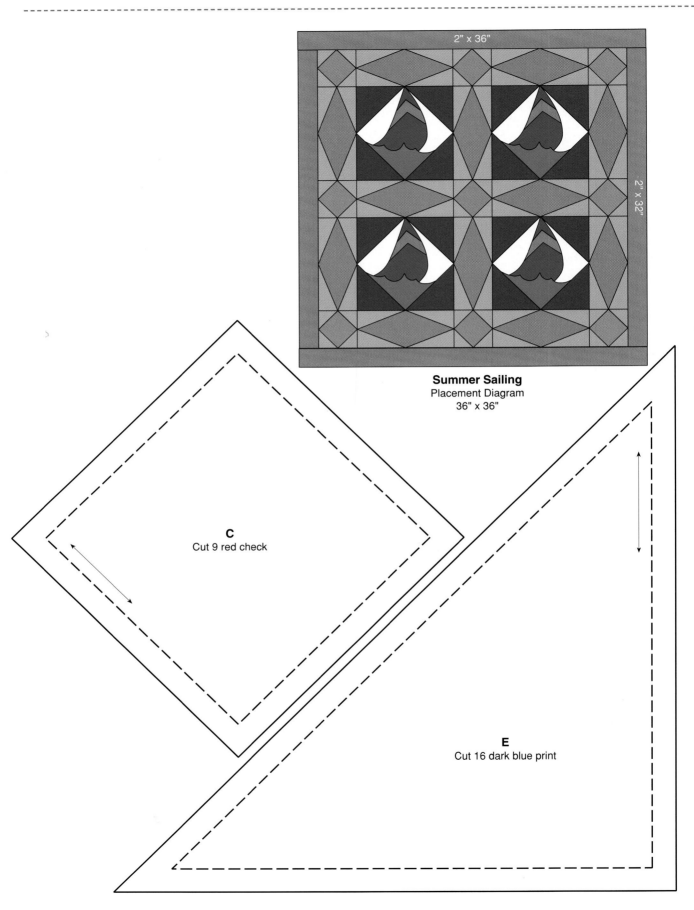

Summer Sailing
Placement Diagram
36" x 36"

C
Cut 9 red check

E
Cut 16 dark blue print

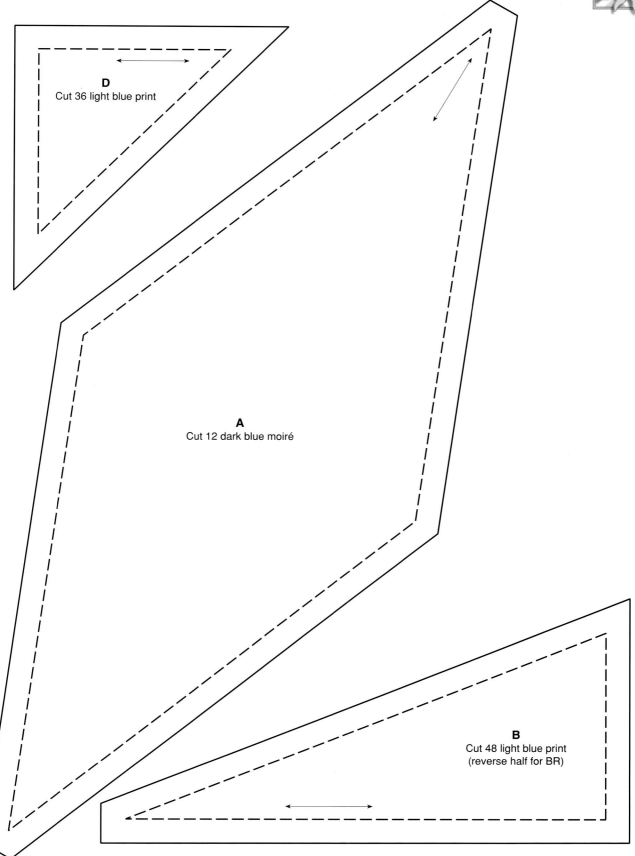

D
Cut 36 light blue print

A
Cut 12 dark blue moiré

B
Cut 48 light blue print
(reverse half for BR)

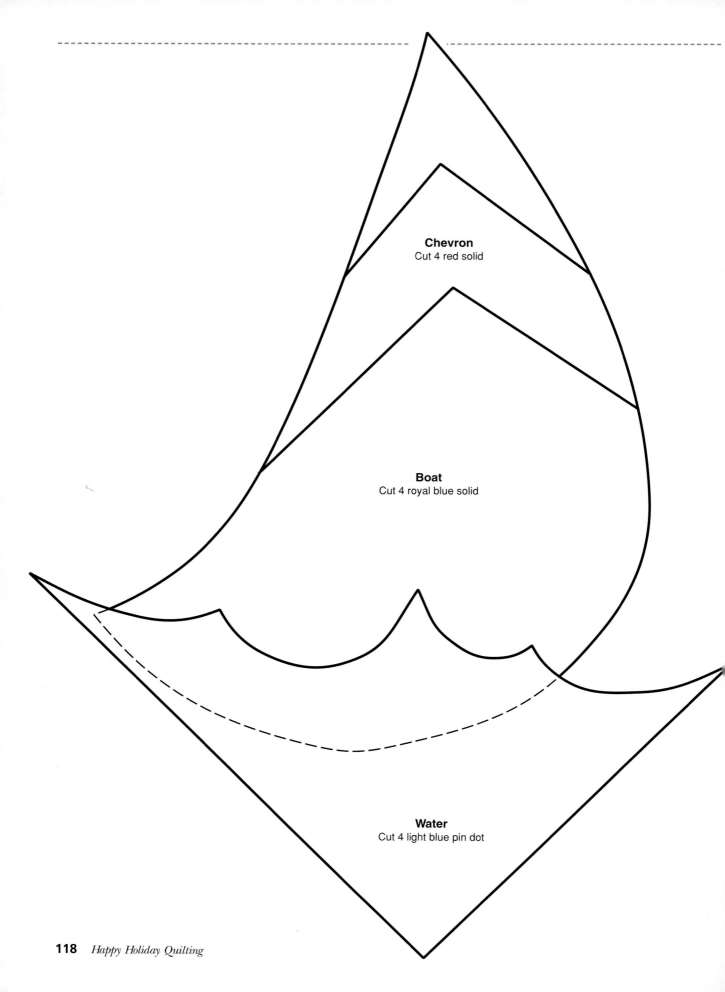

Chevron
Cut 4 red solid

Boat
Cut 4 royal blue solid

Water
Cut 4 light blue pin dot

Summer Vest

By Charlyne Stewart

Make this summery-looking vest using machine appliqué highlighted by machine quilting. Its bright floral design will make any day a holiday.

Specifications

Skill Level: Intermediate

Vest Size: Varies

Materials

Commercial vest pattern

Yardage required for vest and lining listed on pattern

Scraps rose print for flowers

Scraps green print for leaves

1 yard very thin batting

5 1/2 yards self-made or purchased binding

1 spool gold metallic thread

1 spool each green, rose and yellow all-purpose thread

1/2 yard fusible transfer web

Basic sewing supplies and tools, tracing paper, cardboard, template plastic, walking foot and open-toe foot

Instructions

Step 1. Trace patterns for roses, leaves and stems onto tracing paper using pattern pieces given; transfer to cardboard or template plastic. Cut out shapes.

Step 2. Trace shapes onto paper side of fusible transfer web as directed on each piece. Separate shapes, but do not cut on traced lines.

Step 3. Fuse paper shapes to the wrong side of fabric scraps as directed on pattern pieces for colors. Cut out shapes; remove paper backing.

Step 4. Cut vest front and back sections using purchased vest pattern. Cut same-size pieces of batting and lining.

Step 5. Position flowers and leaves on vest front referring to Figure 1, the photo of the finished vest and the Placement Diagram for arrangement suggestions. Fuse shapes in place following manufacturer's instructions.

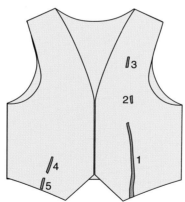

Figure 1
Arrange stem pieces as shown.

Step 6. Layer each front piece with batting and lining pieces. Using an open-toe foot and thread to match appliqué pieces in the top of the machine and thread to match lining in the bobbin, machine-appliqué the pieces in place on both vest fronts. Stitch detail lines marked with dotted lines on pattern pieces; trim loose threads.

Summer Vest
Placement Diagram
Size Varies

Step 7. Using the walking foot and gold metallic thread in the top of the machine and thread to match lining in the bobbin, machine-quilt wavy lines on both vest fronts. Layer the vest back with batting and lining; quilt as for front pieces.

Step 8. Sew the vest front to the vest back at shoulders and side seams. Turn under edges of seams on the inside; hand-stitch in place for a neat finish.

Step 9. Bind sleeve edges with self-made or purchased binding. Beginning at lower edge of back and continuing around vest, bind vest edges with self-made or purchased binding to finish.

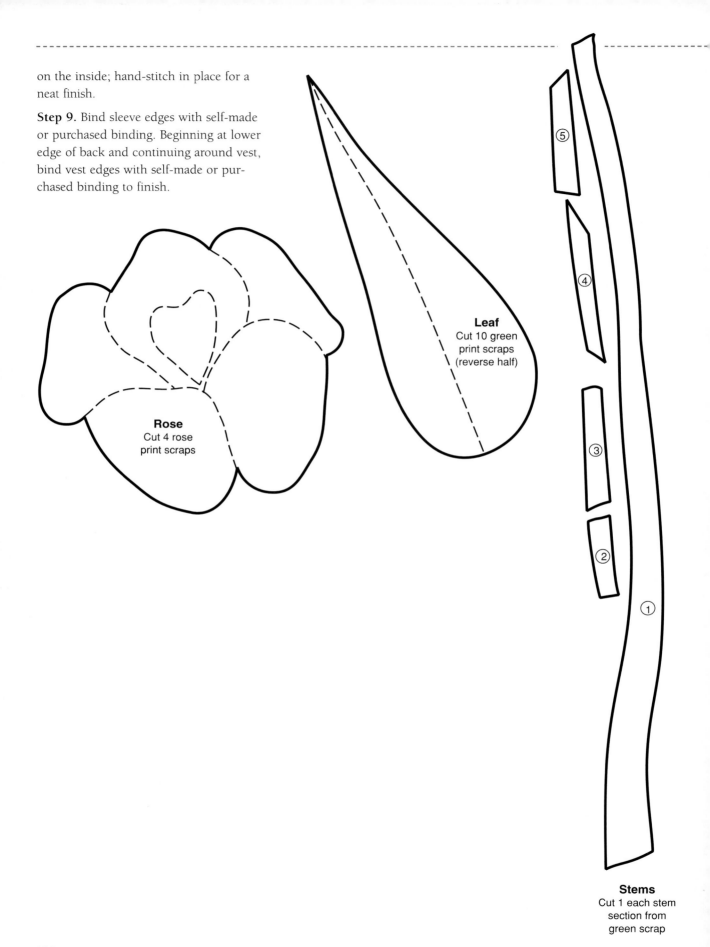

Rose
Cut 4 rose
print scraps

Leaf
Cut 10 green
print scraps
(reverse half)

Stems
Cut 1 each stem
section from
green scrap

Happy Birthday Wall Quilt

By Ann Boyce

Start a new tradition with this colorful birthday quilt. You can hang it year after year and keep it hanging the whole month of the birthday.

Project Specifications

Skill Level: Beginner

Quilt Size: 38" x 38""

Materials

1/8 yard white solid

1/4 yard each light yellow, orange, purple and blue prints

1/2 yard bright yellow print

3/4 yard each pink and lime green prints

Backing 42" x 42"

Batting 42" x 42"

4 1/2 yards self-made or purchased binding

1 1/2 yards pre-pinched white ribbon

1 spool each purple, yellow, orange, pink and blue all-purpose thread

1 spool clear nylon monofilament

1 yard fusible transfer web

1 yard tear-off fabric stabilizer

Basic sewing tools and supplies

Instructions

Step 1. Prepare template for triangle A; cut as directed on piece.

Step 2. Join nine A triangles to make a row as shown in Figure 1; repeat for four rows.

Step 3. Join the rows and trim to 10 1/2" x 12 1/2" as shown in Figure 2.

Figure 1
Join 9 A triangles to make a row.

12 1/2"

10 1/2"

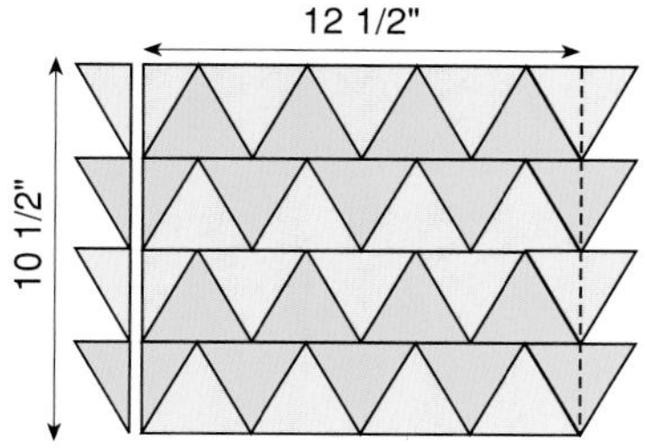

Figure 2
Join the rows as shown;
trim to 10 1/2" x 12 1/2".

Step 4. Sew ribbon trim to trimmed triangle section, leaving 1/4" at top edge and bottom edge for seam as shown in Figure 3. Sew another piece of ribbon trim to top edge below first piece, making loops to the base of each triangle, again referring to Figure 3.

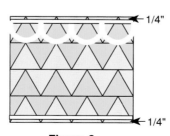

1/4"

1/4"

Figure 3
Sew ribbon trim to trimmed triangle section, leaving 1/4" for seam as shown.

Step 5. Cut two strips pink print 3 1/2" x 10 1/2" and two strips 4 1/2" x 18 1/2".

Step 6. Sew the 10 1/2" strips to opposite sides of pieced triangle section and the 18 1/2" strips to the top and bottom; press seams toward strips.

Step 7. Trace letters onto paper side of fusible web using pattern pieces given. Separate letters and fuse one of each letter to each of the five bright colors. Cut out shapes on traced lines; remove paper.

Step 8. Cut two strips lime green print 5 1/2" x 18 1/2". Sew to opposite sides of decorated center, as in Placement Diagram. Cut two more strips lime green print 5 1/2" x 28 1/2". Sew a strip to top and bottom; press seams toward strips.

Step 9. Center letters to spell PARTY onto lime green print strips, varying positions referring to the Placement Diagram and photo of project for suggestions. Fuse in place following manufacturer's instructions.

Step 10. Trace six candles and six flames onto paper side of fusible transfer web. Cut and fuse to fabrics as directed on patterns as for letters. Cut out; remove paper backing and fuse in place at top of pieced and decorated cake center.

Step 11. Place fabric stabilizer behind letters, candles and flames. Using thread to match fabrics, machine-appliqué pieces in place. When stitching is complete, remove stabilizer and trim threads.

Step 12. Prepare template for triangle B. Cut one strip each purple, orange, blue, bright yellow and pink prints 5 3/4" by fabric width. Cut triangles as directed on piece from cut strips as shown in Figure 4.

Step 13. Join 15 triangles to make a strip referring to Figure 5, arranging colors in a pattern, repeating the same arrangement on strip; repeat for four strips.

Step 14. Sew a strip to each side of the pieced center. Press seams toward strips.

Step 15. Cut two squares purple print 3 7/8" x 3 7/8". Cut each square in half on one diagonal to make D triangles. Cut four C triangles as directed on template. Sew a D triangle to one end of each C triangle to make corner pieces as shown in Figure 6. Sew one corner piece to each end of the two remaining pieced sections. Sew section to top and bottom.

Step 16. Prepare ice cream and cones (four bright yellow print B triangles) as for letters in Step 7. Referring to

Happy Birthday Wall Quilt
Placement Diagram
38" x 38"

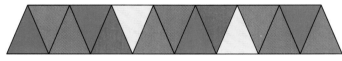

Figure 5
Join triangles to make a border strip as shown.

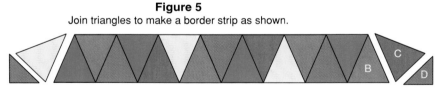

Figure 6
Sew a triangle to end of B for corners.

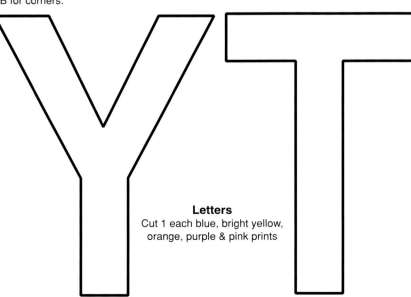

Figure 4
Cut B triangles from
5 3/4"-wide strip as shown.

Placement Diagram, fuse a cone first and an ice cream piece on top at each corner of the pieced center. Place fabric stabilizer under shapes. Machine-appliqué pieces in place using matching thread. Remove stabilizer and trim threads.

Step 17. Prepare quilt top for quilting and finish referring to General Instructions. *Note: Quilt was machine-quilted using monofilament thread.*

Letters
Cut 1 each blue, bright yellow, orange, purple & pink prints

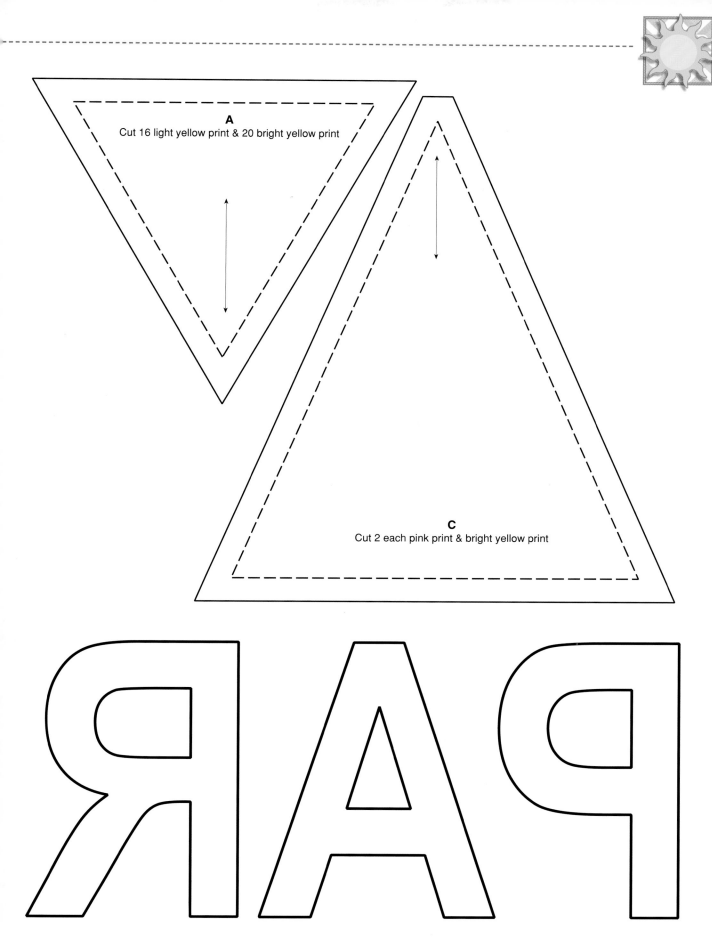

A
Cut 16 light yellow print & 20 bright yellow print

C
Cut 2 each pink print & bright yellow print

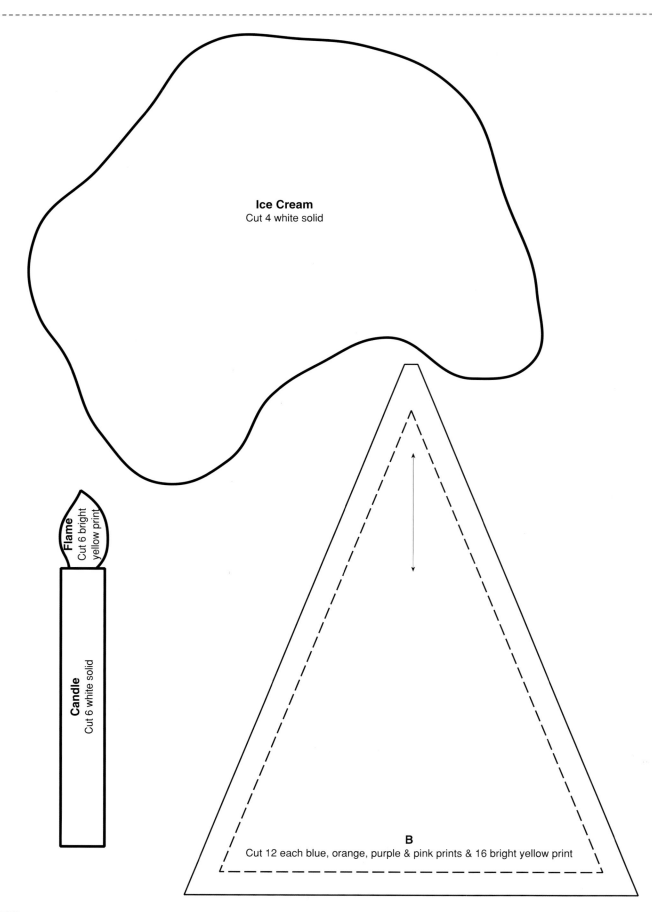

Ice Cream
Cut 4 white solid

Flame
Cut 6 bright
yellow print

Candle
Cut 6 white solid

B
Cut 12 each blue, orange, purple & pink prints & 16 bright yellow print

My Grandpa's Bow Ties

By Jill Reber

I designed this quilt in honor of my Grandpa Wiseman who often wore bow ties. I chose reproduction shirting-style prints for the backgrounds and plaids for the bow ties. Adding shirt buttons gives the quilt an appearance of real shirts and bow ties when the quilt is hung on point.

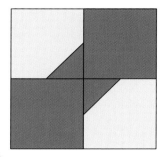

Bow Tie
6" x 6" Block

Specifications

Skill Level: Beginner

Wall Quilt Size: 35" x 35"

Block Size: 6" x 6"

Number of Blocks: 16

Materials

1 strip each 3 1/2" x 44" of 8 different plaids for ties

1 strip each 3 1/2" x 44" of 8 different shirting prints

1/2 yard blue plaid for outside borders

Backing 39" x 39"

Batting 39" x 39"

4 1/8 yards self-made or purchased binding

All-purpose thread to match fabrics

Basic sewing supplies and tools, rotary cutter, ruler and cutting mat

Project Note

My Grandpa's Bow Ties was designed to hang on point. The placement of the buttons on the shirting fabric gives the appearance of a shirt and bow tie.

Instructions

Step 1. From each plaid strip cut four 3 1/2" x 3 1/2" squares for 32 A

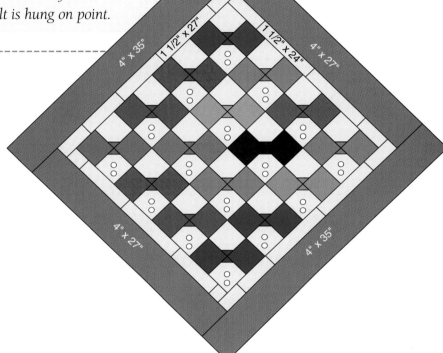

My Grandpa's Bow Ties
Placement Diagram
35" x 35"

squares and four 2 3/8" x 2 3/8" squares; cut these squares on one diagonal to make 32 B triangles.

Step 2. From each shirting strip cut four 3 1/2" x 3 1/2" squares, to make 32 A squares.

Step 3. Place the C triangle on one corner of two matching shirting squares. Mark and cut off corner as shown in Figure 1. Sew a B triangle to each of these A pieces.

Step 4. Join two matching A squares with matching shirting squares as shown in Figure 2 to complete one block; repeat for 16 blocks.

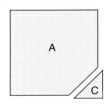

Figure 1
Cut 1 corner off shirting A squares.

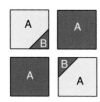

Figure 2
Join pieces to
complete 1 block.

Step 5. Arrange blocks in four rows of four blocks each referring to the Placement Diagram and photo for positioning of blocks; join in rows and press. Join rows; press.

Step 6. Cut remaining shirting fabrics into 2"-wide strips of various lengths. Join strips on short ends to make two 2" x 24 1/2" strips for top and bottom and two 2" x 27 1/2" strips for sides. Sew strips to pieced center; press seams toward strips.

Step 7. Cut two strips blue plaid 4 1/2" x 27 1/2"; sew a strip to top and bottom of pieced center. Press seams toward strips. Cut two strips blue plaid 4 1/2" x 35 1/2"; sew a strip to opposite sides of pieced center. Press seams toward strips.

Step 8. Prepare for quilting referring to General Instructions.

Step 9. Quilt as desired by hand or machine. The quilt shown was quilted in one continuous line as shown in Figure 3. When quilting is complete trim edges even. Bind with self-made or purchased binding.

Step 10. Sew two matching buttons on bottom right corner of each block as shown in Figure 4 to finish.

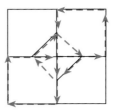

Figure 3
Quilt each block as shown.

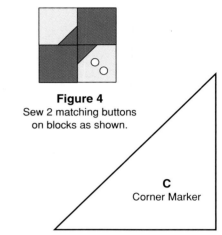

Figure 4
Sew 2 matching buttons
on blocks as shown.

C
Corner Marker

Autumn Occasions

*E*njoy the excitement and sounds of autumn with quilts celebrating Halloween, Thanksgiving and Columbus Day. Celebrate special occasions by stitching a floral wreath of flowers in autumn colors. Or stitch a quilt with hunting as its theme. Then end the year by making a quilt that includes every member of the family on a tree full of button photos.

Celebrate the changing colors of the leaves, the crisp fall air and a cozy cabin in the woods with this quilt combining scrappy Log Cabin blocks and Bear Paw blocks. Add a border of freezer-paper appliqué bears, log cabins of scraps and pieced trees to complete this quilt. It's a perfect gift for your favorite hunter or use it to decorate a cabin retreat or a den. *Bear Paw Cabin* pattern begins on page 132.

Bear Paw Quilt

By Christine Schultz

This scrappy quilt uses the Bear Paw block with Log Cabin centers. It is a perfect lap quilt for cold autumn and winter days when it gets dark early and nap time comes around.

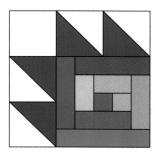

Bear Paw
7 1/2" x 7 1/2"
Make 24

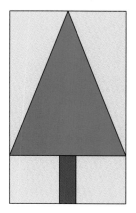

Evergreen Tree
3 1/2" x 6"
Make 13

Specifications

Skill Level: Intermediate

Quilt Size: 52 1/2" x 72 1/2"

Block Size: 3 1/2" x 6", 5" x 6" and 7 1/2" x 7 1/2"

Number of Blocks: 7 Cabins, 13 Evergreen Trees and 24 Bear Paws

Materials

Assorted brown scraps for bears

Red print scraps for cabin doors

1/3 yard green print for trees

1/2 yard assorted brown scraps for cabin logs and tree trunks

2 yards dark brown print

2 yards white-and-brown print

1 yard assorted fabric scraps cut into 1 1/2"-wide strips for Log Cabin blocks

1 1/2 yards tan print for outer borders

Batting 57" x 77"

Backing 57" x 77"

7 1/2 yards self-made or purchased binding

Neutral color all-purpose thread

1 spool off-white quilting thread

Freezer paper

Basic sewing tools and supplies

Making Pieced Center

Step 1. Cut 1 1/2"-wide strips from scraps for Log Cabin blocks. From some of these strips cut 1 1/2" x

1 1/2" squares for block centers; you will need 48 squares.

Step 2. Sew two 1 1/2" x 1 1/2" squares together; repeat for 24 units. *Note: Unlike traditional Log Cabin blocks, the color placement in these blocks is totally random.*

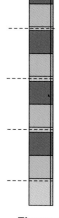

Step 3. Sew a strip of any color to the right side of the pieced unit; press seam toward strip. Trim strip even with squares as shown in Figure 1.

Figure 1
Trim strip even with squares.

Step 4. Continuing in a counter-clockwise direction, add strips around center until there are two strips on each side of the center square; trim as in Step 3. When stitching is complete, the unit should measure 5 1/2" x 5 1/2"; repeat for 24 Log Cabin units.

Step 5. Cut 24 strips white-and-brown print 3" x 8" and 24 squares 3" x 3"; set aside. Cut five strips white-and-brown print 3 3/8" by fabric width. Cut each strip into 3 3/8" segments. Cut each segment on the diagonal to make triangles. You will need 96 triangles. Repeat with dark brown print for 96 triangles.

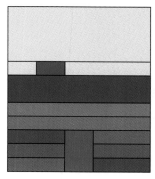

Cabin
5" x 6"
Make 7

Step 6. Sew a dark brown print triangle to a white print triangle to make triangle/squares. *Note: See special instructions for alternate method of making quick-pieced squares on page 135.* You will need 96 units.

Step 7. Join two triangle/squares to make A and B units as shown in Figure 2; repeat for 24 of each set.

6" x 6"

1 1/2" x 37 1/2"

2 1/2" x 17 1/2"

11/2" x 60 1/2"

Bear Paw Cabin
Placement Diagram
52 1/2" x 72 1/2"

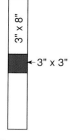

Step 11. Join two blocks with a 3" x 8" white-and-brown print rectangle to make block row as shown in Figure 6; press seams toward rectangle. Repeat for 12 block rows.

3" x 8"

3" x 3"

Figure 5
Sew a 3" x 8" rectangle to opposite sides of the square.

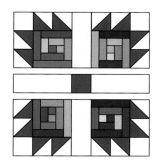

3" x 8"

Figure 6
Join 2 blocks with a 3" x 8" rectangle.

Step 12. Join two block rows with a sashing row to complete one block as shown in Figure 7. Press seams toward sashing row; repeat for six blocks.

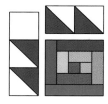

Figure 7
Join 2 block rows with a sashing row as shown.

Step 13. Cut seven strips 3" x 18" white-and-brown print. Join two strips with a 3" x 3" dark brown print square to make a sashing row; repeat for two rows. Join two blocks with one 3" x 18" strip to make a block row; repeat for three block rows. Press all seams toward strips.

Step 14. Join block rows with sashing rows to complete pieced center.

Step 8. Add a 3" x 3" white-and-brown print square to the end of a B unit as shown in Figure 3.

Step 9. Sew the pieced units to the Log Cabin units as shown in Figure 4; repeat for 24 blocks.

Step 10. Cut eight squares dark brown print 3" x 3". Sew a white-and-brown print 3" x 8" rectangle cut in Step 5 to opposite sides of one square to make sashing row as shown in Figure 5; press seams toward squares. Repeat for six units. Set aside remaining squares.

A Unit

B Unit

Figure 2
Join triangles to make an A and B unit as shown.

Figure 3
Sew a white-and-brown print square to the end of a B unit.

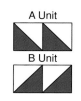

Figure 4
Sew the pieced units to a Log Cabin unit as shown.

Step 15. Cut two strips dark brown print 2" x 38". Sew strips to top and bottom of pieced center; press seams toward strips. Cut two strips 2" x 61"; sew to opposite sides. Press seams toward strips.

Making Evergreen Tree Blocks

Step 1. Prepare templates A and B using pattern pieces given. Cut as directed on each piece.

Step 2. Cut one strip brown print 1" by fabric width and two strips tan print 2" by fabric width. Sew the brown strip between the two tan print strips; press seams toward brown print strip. Cut into 2"-wide segments; you will need 13 segments.

Step 3. Sew B and BR to A; repeat for 13 units. Sew a unit cut in Step 2 to the bottom of each A-B unit to complete one Evergreen Tree block as shown in Figure 8; repeat for 13 blocks.

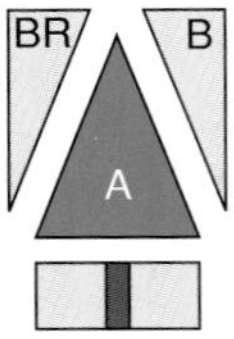

Figure 8
Piece 1 Evergreen Tree
block as shown.

Making Cabin Blocks

Step 1. Cut 42 rectangles 1" x 2 1/2" from brown scraps. Sew together on long sides in sets of three. Cut seven 1 1/2" x 2" rectangles from red scraps; sew a pieced brown unit to each 2" side of each red scrap rectangle to make door unit as shown in Figure 9. Repeat for seven units.

Step 2. From brown scraps, cut 14 strips 1" x 5 1/2" and seven strips 1 1/2" x 5 1/2". Sew two 1" strips to one 1 1/2" strip as shown in Figure 10; repeat for seven units. Sew one of these units to one long side of the pre-

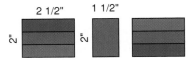

Figure 9
Make door unit as shown.

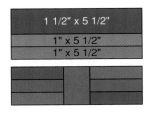

Figure 10
Stitch pieces together as shown.

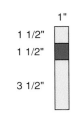

Figure 11
Make a chimney unit as shown.

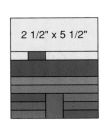

Figure 12
Complete a Cabin block
as shown.

viously pieced unit as shown in Figure 10; repeat for seven units.

Step 3. Cut seven chimney units 1" x 1 1/2" rust scraps. Cut seven pieces each tan print 1" x 1 1/2" and 1" x 3 1/2". Sew a rust scrap piece between one of each size tan print pieces to make chimney unit as shown in Figure 11; repeat for seven units. Sew one unit to the top of previously pieced units.

Step 4. Cut seven strips tan print 2 1/2" x 5 1/2". Sew one strip to top of a pieced unit to complete one block as shown in Figure 12; repeat for seven blocks.

Piecing Borders

Step 1. For top border strip, cut one piece tan print 6 1/2" x 17", one piece 6 1/2" x 15" and one piece 1 1/2" x 6 1/2". Join one Cabin block and one Evergreen Tree block with the 1 1/2" x 6 1/2" strip. Sew the 17" strip to the Cabin-block side and the

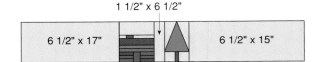

Figure 13
Piece top border as shown.

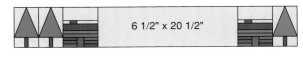

Figure 14
Piece bottom border as shown.

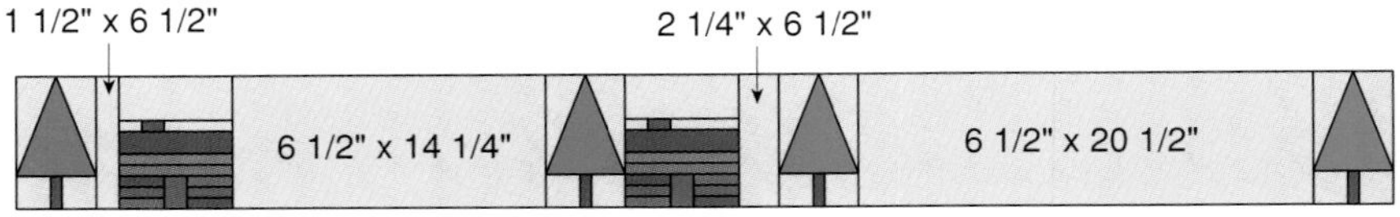

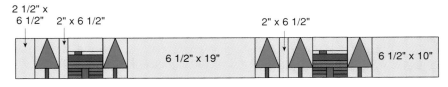

Figure 15
Piece left side border as shown.

Figure 16
Piece right side border as shown.

15" strip to the Evergreen-block side as shown in Figure 13. Press strip. Sew to top of pieced center; press seams toward border strip.

Step 2. For bottom border strip, cut one piece tan print 6 1/2" x 20 1/2". Join pieces in this order: two Evergreen Tree blocks, Cabin block, 6 1/2" x 20 1/2" piece, Cabin block and Evergreen Tree block as shown in Figure 14. Sew to bottom of pieced center; press seams toward strips.

Step 3. For left side border strip, cut one piece each tan print 6 1/2" x 14 1/4", 6 1/2" x 20 1/2", 1 1/2" x 6 1/2" and 2 1/4" x 6 1/2". Arrange the pieces with four Evergreen Tree blocks and two Cabin blocks referring to Figure 15; sew together to complete strip. Cut four squares tan print 6 1/2" x 6 1/2". Sew one of

these squares to each end of the strip. Sew to left side of pieced center; press seams toward strip.

Step 4. For right side border strip, cut one piece each tan print 2 1/2" x 6 1/2", 6 1/2" x 19" and 6 1/2" x 10" and two strips 2" x 6 1/2". Arrange the strips with two Cabin blocks and five Evergreen Tree blocks referring to Figure 16; sew together to complete strip. Sew a 6 1/2" x 6 1/2" tan print square to each end. Sew to right side of pieced center; press seams toward strip.

Freezer Paper Bears

Step 1. Prepare template for bear shape. Trace bear shapes on dull side of freezer paper. Cut bears on traced lines. Iron freezer paper shapes, shiny side down, onto wrong side of scraps for bears.

Step 2. When paper is fused to fabric, let cool. Cut bear shape from fabric, cutting outside traced lines to leave a turn-under seam allowance of about 3/16".

Step 3. Place bear, right side up, on border at chosen location referring to the Placement Diagram and photo of quilt for suggestions; pin in place. Using a sharp needle and matching thread, stitch bear in place, turning under edge of fabric over freezer paper as you stitch. When stitching is complete, carefully slit the back of the border behind the bear patch and gently remove the freezer paper; press. Repeat for seven bears.

Finishing

Step 1. Prepare pieced top for quilting and finish referring to the General Instructions.

Quick-Pieced Squares

Note: Using this method assures a more accurate 3 1/2" pieced square without wrestling with a diagonal bias seam.

Step 1. Cut one piece each white-and-brown print and dark brown print 15" x 22". On the wrong side of the white-and-brown print, mark a grid of 24 (3 3/8" x 3 3/8") squares. Draw a diagonal line through each square, alternating the direction of the diagonals as shown in Figure 1.

Step 2. Layer the marked fabric with the dark brown print piece right sides together; pin layers to hold.

Step 3. Stitch 1/4" on each side of each diagonal line as shown in Figure 2. **Note:** Alternating the direction of the diagonals allows you to stitch continuously from one square to the next.

Step 4. Carefully cut squares in the grid apart with a rotary cutter. Cut each square in half on the drawn diagonal lines as shown in Figure 3. Each square will yield two triangular units, which when opened will be a pieced 3 1/2" (3" finished) square. Press seam allowances toward brown print triangle side.

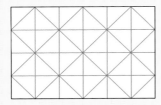

Figure 1
Mark a grid on fabric as shown.

Figure 2
Stitch 1/4" on each side of diagonal lines.

Figure 3
Cut each square in half on diagonal lines.

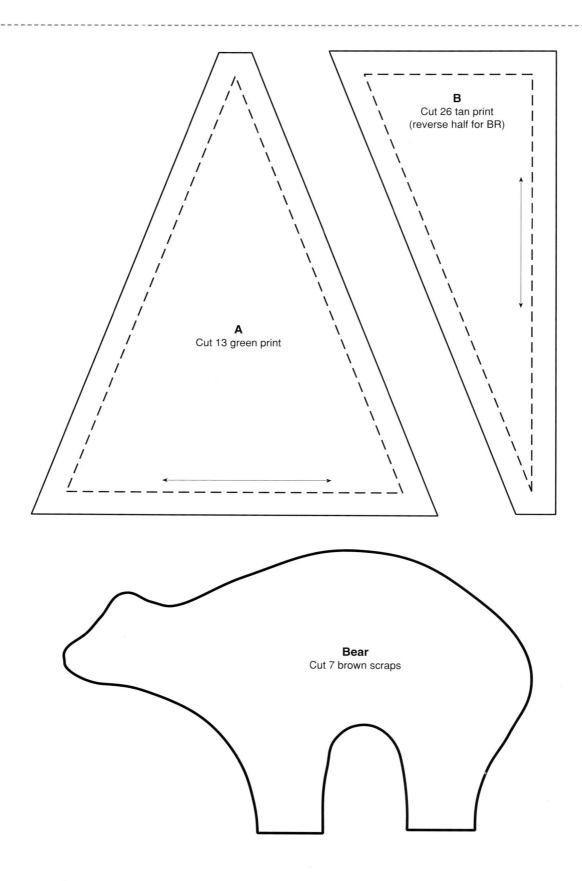

A
Cut 13 green print

B
Cut 26 tan print
(reverse half for BR)

Bear
Cut 7 brown scraps

Sunflower Sensation

By Lucy A. Fazely

Surround star shapes with yellow and they look like sunflowers. Make this quick and easy wall quilt using stripe fabric in the stars and borders for a coordinated look.

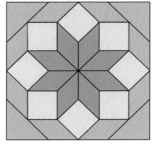

Eight-Pointed Star
19 1/4" x 19 1/4" Block

Specifications

Skill Level: Advanced Beginner

Quilt Size: 52 1/2" x 52 1/2"

Block Size: 19 1/4" x 19 1/4"

Number of Blocks: 4

Materials

3/4 yard yellow pastel print

1 1/4 yards green pastel print

3 yards green border print

Backing 57" x 57"

Batting 57" x 57"

6 1/2 yards self-made or purchased binding

Neutral color all-purpose thread

Basic sewing tools and supplies

Instructions

Step 1. Prepare template for A using pattern piece given. Cut as directed on pattern piece. *Note: The template was placed in the exact same motif on the stripe for eight A pieces. It was then moved to another location on the stripe for eight more pieces. This process was repeated for four different sets of eight identical A pieces.*

Step 2. Cut 32 squares yellow pastel print 4 1/2" x 4 1/2" for B.

Step 3. From green pastel print, cut eight squares 7" x 7". Cut each square in half on one diagonal to make 16 C triangles.

Step 4. Keeping the same design in each star, join two A pieces as shown

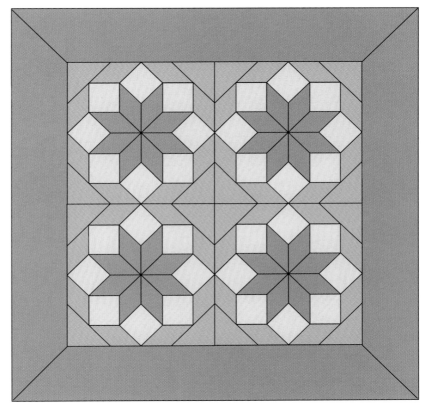

Sunflower Sensation
Placement Diagram
52 1/2" x 52 1/2"

in Figure 1, starting and stopping stitching at seam line; repeat for four units. Press all seams in one direction. Join two units to make half a star design; repeat for second half.

Figure 1
Join 2 A pieces, starting and stopping stitching at dots.

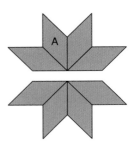

Figure 2
Join 2 halves to make a star design.

Join the two halves to complete the star unit as shown in Figure 2.

Step 5. Set in B squares between star points as shown in Figure 3; press seams away from yellow squares.

Step 6. Set in green pastel print A pieces as shown in Figure 4. Sew a C triangle to each corner to complete one block. Trim C triangles even with edge of block as shown in Figure 5; repeat for four blocks.

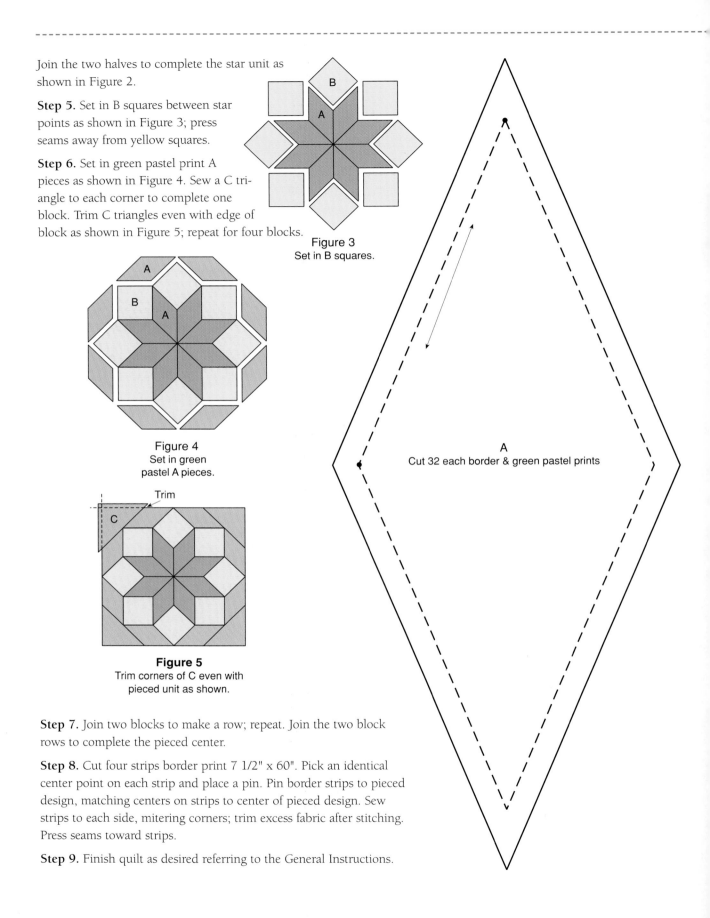

Figure 3
Set in B squares.

Figure 4
Set in green
pastel A pieces.

Trim

Figure 5
Trim corners of C even with
pieced unit as shown.

A
Cut 32 each border & green pastel prints

Step 7. Join two blocks to make a row; repeat. Join the two block rows to complete the pieced center.

Step 8. Cut four strips border print 7 1/2" x 60". Pick an identical center point on each strip and place a pin. Pin border strips to pieced design, matching centers on strips to center of pieced design. Sew strips to each side, mitering corners; trim excess fabric after stitching. Press seams toward strips.

Step 9. Finish quilt as desired referring to the General Instructions.

Columbus Sets Sail

By Michele Crawford

This small wall quilt commemorates Columbus and his discovery trips. The appliquéd sailboats and compass designs combine with the sailboat print to make a pleasing project.

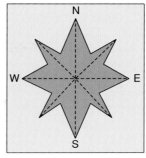

Compass
8" x 9" Block

Specifications

Skill Level: Beginner

Quilt Size: 19" x 21"

Block Size: 8" x 9"

Number of Blocks: 4

Materials

1/2 yard cream print

1/8 yard dark tan print

1/8 yard medium blue mottled

1/6 yard navy sailboat print

8" x 8" square gold print

1" x 3" piece red solid

7" x 17" piece white-on-white print

Quilter's fleece 23" x 25"

Backing 23" x 25"

2 1/2 yards self-made or purchased binding

1/2 yard fusible transfer web

1 spool each gray, brown and neutral color all-purpose thread

1 spool gold metallic thread

1 yard 6-strand navy embroidery floss

Gold Star Button

Basic sewing tools and supplies

Columbus Sets Sail
Placement Diagram
19" x 21"

Sailboat Blocks

Step 1. From cream print, cut three rectangles 6 3/4" x 8 1/2" and three squares 2 3/8" x 2 3/8". Cut squares in half on one diagonal to make A triangles.

Step 2. From dark tan print, cut three rectangles 2" x 5 1/2" for B and three squares 2 3/8" x 2 3/8". Cut squares in half on one diagonal to make A triangles.

Step 3. From blue mottled fabric, cut three rectangles 1 3/4" x 8 1/2" for C.

Step 4. Sew a dark tan print A triangle to a cream print A triangle to make a square; repeat for six squares. Sew an A-A unit to each end of B as shown in Figure 1.

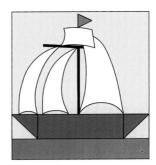

Sailboat
8" x 9" Block

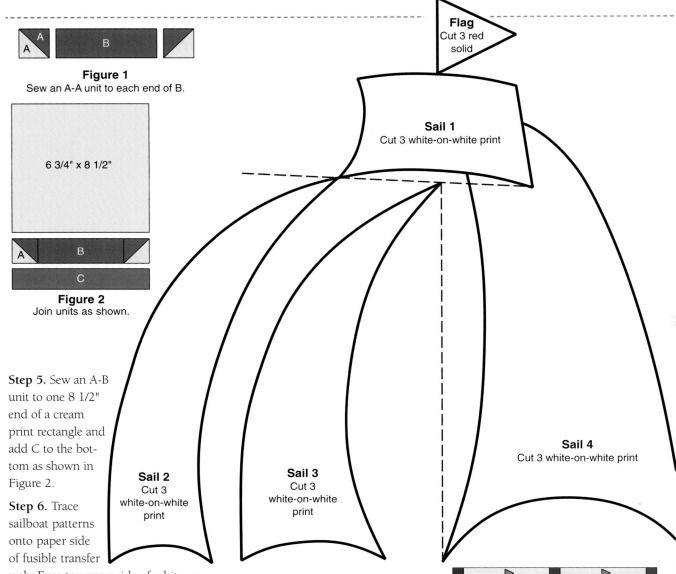

Figure 1
Sew an A-A unit to each end of B.

6 3/4" x 8 1/2"

Figure 2
Join units as shown.

Flag
Cut 3 red solid

Sail 1
Cut 3 white-on-white print

Sail 2
Cut 3 white-on-white print

Sail 3
Cut 3 white-on-white print

Sail 4
Cut 3 white-on-white print

Step 5. Sew an A-B unit to one 8 1/2" end of a cream print rectangle and add C to the bottom as shown in Figure 2.

Step 6. Trace sailboat patterns onto paper side of fusible transfer web. Fuse to wrong side of white-on-white print; cut out on traced lines. Remove paper backing.

Step 7. Trace flag shape onto paper side of fusible transfer web. Fuse to 1" x 3" piece red solid; cut out on traced lines. Remove paper backing.

Step 8. Arrange sail pieces and flag on cream print area of pieced block referring to the Placement Diagram for positioning. Fuse in place; repeat for three blocks.

Compass Block

Step 1. Trace Compass design onto paper side of fusible transfer web. Fuse to wrong side of gold print fabric; cut out on traced lines. Remove paper backing.

Step 2. Cut a rectangle cream print 8 1/2" x 9 1/2". Center the Compass design on the rectangle; fuse in place.

Assembly

Step 1. Cut six strips each 1 1/2" x 8 1/2" and 1 1/2" x 9 1/2" navy print. *Note: If the print has a directional design, be sure to cut strips in the right direction for horizontal and vertical strips.*

Step 2. Cut nine 1 1/2" x 1 1/2" squares blue mottled fabric.

Step 3. Join two Sailboat blocks with three 1 1/2"x 9 1/2" strips as shown in Figure 3. Repeat with one Sailboat and the Compass block. Press seams toward strips.

Figure 3
Join 2 Sailboat blocks with 3 sashing strips to make a block row.

Step 4. Join two 1 1/2" x 8 1/2" strips with three 1 1/2" x 1 1/2" squares as shown in Figure 4; repeat for three rows.

Step 5. Join the block rows with the sashing rows as shown in Figure 5; press seams toward strips.

Step 6. Prepare completed top for quilting and quilt referring to the General Instructions.

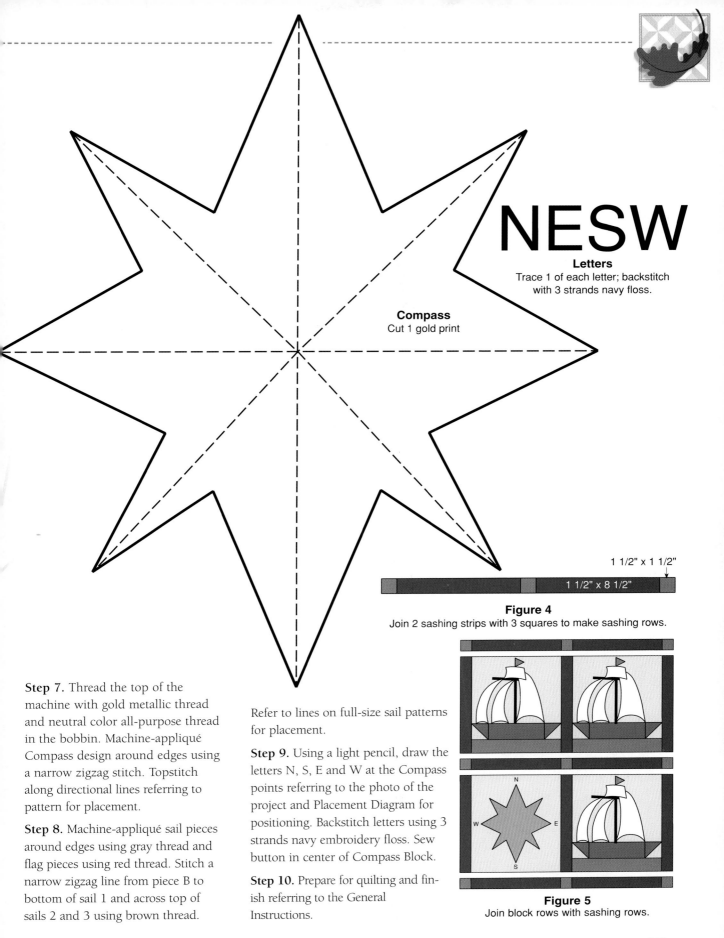

NESW
Letters
Trace 1 of each letter; backstitch
with 3 strands navy floss.

Compass
Cut 1 gold print

1 1/2" x 1 1/2"

1 1/2" x 8 1/2"

Figure 4
Join 2 sashing strips with 3 squares to make sashing rows.

Figure 5
Join block rows with sashing rows.

Step 7. Thread the top of the machine with gold metallic thread and neutral color all-purpose thread in the bobbin. Machine-appliqué Compass design around edges using a narrow zigzag stitch. Topstitch along directional lines referring to pattern for placement.

Step 8. Machine-appliqué sail pieces around edges using gray thread and flag pieces using red thread. Stitch a narrow zigzag line from piece B to bottom of sail 1 and across top of sails 2 and 3 using brown thread.

Refer to lines on full-size sail patterns for placement.

Step 9. Using a light pencil, draw the letters N, S, E and W at the Compass points referring to the photo of the project and Placement Diagram for positioning. Backstitch letters using 3 strands navy embroidery floss. Sew button in center of Compass Block.

Step 10. Prepare for quilting and finish referring to the General Instructions.

Family Tree Anniversary Quilt

By Wendy Kinzler

Genealogy buffs will love this little family tree quilt. Make in celebration of your wedding anniversary. As your family grows, just add more photo buttons.

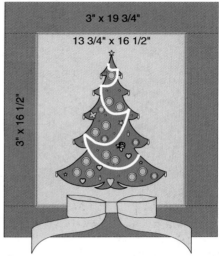

Family Tree Anniversary Quilt
Placement Diagram
19 3/4" x 22 1/2"

Specifications

Skill Level: Intermediate
Quilt Size: 19 3/4" x 22 1/2"

Materials

12" x 15" piece blue print for tree

1/2 yard multicolored sky print for background

1/4 yard dark floral print for borders

Backing 22" x 25"

Thin Batting 22" x 25"

2 1/2 yards self-made or purchased binding

12" x 15" piece fusible transfer web

1 3/4 yards 1/4"-thick gold rope trim

3/4 yard 1 1/2"-wide gold ribbon

7/8" flat buttons with rims

Photos to fit buttons

4 mm faux pearls, assorted beads, charms and other embellishments

Tacky glue or glue gun and glue sticks.

Neutral color all-purpose thread

1 spool white cotton-covered polyester thread

1 spool white heavy-duty thread

1 yard gold metallic 6-strand embroidery floss

Basic sewing tools and supplies

Instructions

Step 1. Make tree pattern enlarging pattern given in Figure 1.

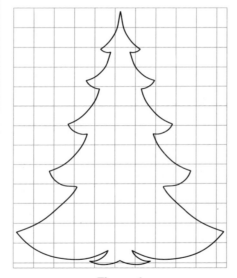

Figure 1
Enlarge to make tree pattern; 1 square equals 1". Cut 1 tree shape from blue print.

Step 2. Trace tree shape onto paper side of fusible transfer web. Fuse to wrong side of tree fabric. Cut out; remove paper backing. Fold tree and crease to mark center.

Step 3. Cut a rectangle 14 1/4" x 17" from multicolored sky print. Fold and crease to mark center.

Step 4. Center tree on background piece; fuse in place following manufacturer's instructions.

Step 5. Cut two strips dark floral print 3 1/2" x 17"; sew to opposite long sides of appliquéd center. Press seams toward strips. Cut two more strips dark floral print 3 1/2" x 20 1/4"; sew to top and bottom. Press seams toward strips.

Step 6. Prepare top for quilting and finish referring to General Instructions.

Embellishing

Step 1. Thread strings of 4 mm pearls onto cotton-covered white polyester thread. Attach ends securely to tree, referring to photo of quilt for placement suggestions.

Step 2. Make a template to fit center of buttons. From this make a window template. Center over photos before marking to cut. *Note: Practice this on a scrap piece of paper marked with an X before cutting photos to see if the size works.*

Step 3. Thread a 10" piece of heavy-duty thread through holes in button, leave two ends hanging at back. Glue photos to button. Fasten to tree, tying

Continued on page 161

Cobweb

By Lucy A. Fazely

Use a narrow colorful stripe to create the web sections
of this fascinating quilt. Be careful when sewing as
this one can be hard on the eyes.

Cobweb
6" x 6" Block

Specifications

Skill Level: Beginner

Quilt Size: 19" x 19"

Block Size: 6" x 6"

Number of Blocks: 9

Materials

1/3 yard each blue and red solids

1 yard narrow stripe

Backing 23" x 23"

Lightweight batting 23" x 23"

Neutral color all-purpose thread

Optional toy spider

Optional plastic or wooden clothes hanger

Basic sewing tools and supplies

Instructions

Step 1. Prepare templates using pattern pieces given. Mark line on A for matching when cutting.

Step 2. Cut four strips 3" x 36" and one strip 3" x 18 from narrow stripe with stripe running the length of the strips.

Step 3. Cut nine strips each red and blue solids 2" x 18". Sew a red and blue solid strip to long edge of each 3" x 36" stripe strip as shown in Figure 1. Sew a red strip to one side and a blue strip to the opposite side of the 3" x 18" strip as shown in Figure 2. Press seams toward red or blue strips.

Step 4. From each 6" x 36" strip section, cut eight A pieces—four with red tips and four with blue tips as shown in Figure 3. Repeat on 4" x 18" strip as shown in Figure 4.

Step 5. Sew a red-point A to a blue-point A; repeat for four units. Join two units together to make halves. Join halves to make a circle; repeat for nine units and press seams in the same direction.

Step 6. Cut B pieces from stripe referring to Figure 5 for placement on stripe. Lay out A units on a flat surface. Place B triangles at corners of each unit matching stripes on B pieces to make a square design at block intersections as shown in Figure 6. Pin B pieces to A units and stitch.

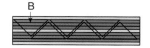

Figure 5
Cut B triangles from strips as shown.

Intersection of B pieces

Figure 6
Position B pieces so they make a
design at intersections as shown.

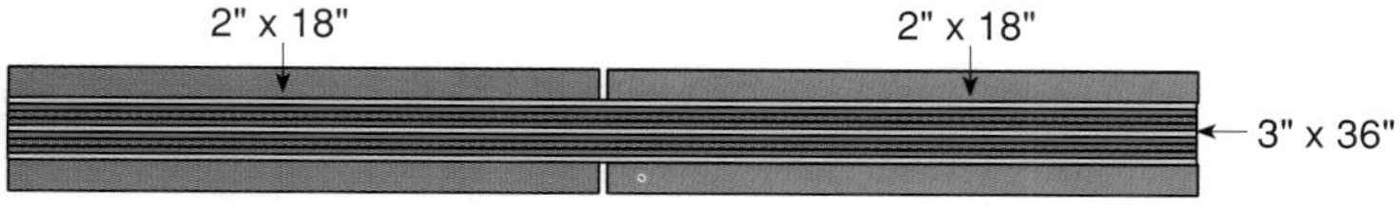

Figure 1
Join strips as shown.

Figure 2
Join strips as shown.

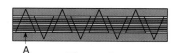

Figure 4
Lay A template on strip-pieced sections as shown.

Figure 3
Lay A template on strip-pieced sections as shown.

Step 7. Lay blocks out again to form pattern; join three blocks to make a row. Repeat for three rows; press.

Step 8. Prepare top for quilting referring to General Instructions.

Step 9. Machine-quilt in the ditch of all seams with contrasting thread.

Step 10. When quilting is complete, trim backing 2" larger than quilt top all around. Trim batting 1/2" larger than quilt top all around. Turn under edge of backing 1/4". Fold backing even with batting edge to front. Stitch in place on front side by hand or machine to finish edge.

Step 11. Hand-stitch a plastic or wooden clothes hanger on the diagonal of one corner on the backside for hanging. Sew the optional spider to one corner on the bottom front corner of the quilt to finish.

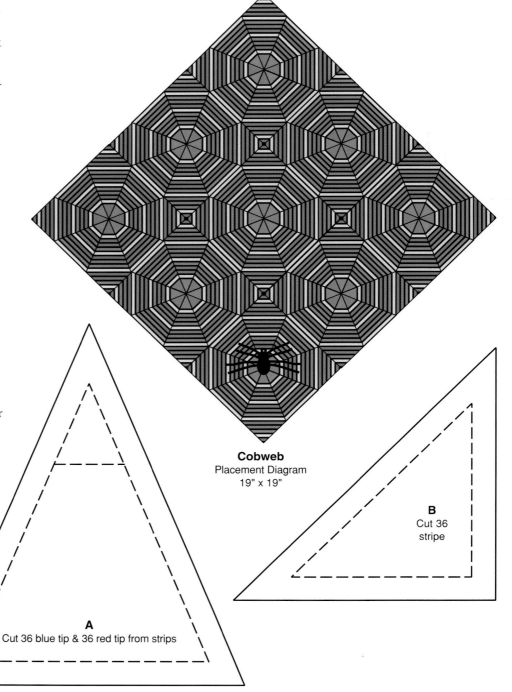

Cobweb
Placement Diagram
19" x 19"

B
Cut 36
stripe

A
Cut 36 blue tip & 36 red tip from strips

Autumn Wreath

By Jodi G. Warner

Combine the colors of autumn with pieced leaves to make this small wall quilt. Hang it in your entry or on your door in celebration of the autumn season.

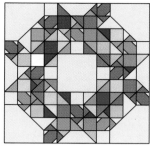

Wreath
13 3/4" x 13 3/4" Block

Leaf
4 1/4" x 4 1/4" Block

Specifications

Skill Level: Advanced

Quilt Size: 19 1/4" x 29 1/4"

Block Size: 4 1/4" x 4 1/4" and 13 3/4" x 13 3/4"

Number of Blocks: 1 large and 6 small

Materials

Scraps various autumn-colored prints and solids including tan, beige, rust, plum, burgundy, mauve, rose, medium pink, cream, light, medium and dark blue, navy and goldenrod

1/8 yard taupe solid

1/4 yard light pink solid

1/2 yard each gray print and burgundy stripe

Backing 23" x 33"

Batting 23" x 33"

3 yards self-made or purchased binding

Neutral color all-purpose thread

Brown and cream quilting thread

Basic sewing tools and supplies

Instructions

Step 1. Prepare templates using pattern pieces given. Cut as directed on each piece.

Step 2. Sew an E triangle to each side of D to complete a square as shown in Figure 1; repeat for 12 units, referring to Figure 7 for color arrangement. *Note: The number to cut for each piece is given with a notation about colors used on sample. It is suggested you choose your own color arrangement rather than try to copy the sample exactly.*

Figure 1
Sew 2 E triangles to D.

Step 3. Sew C to C to B as shown in Figure 2, making color arrangements as shown in Figure 7; repeat for 13 units. Sew B to B as shown in Figure 3, again referring to Figure 7; repeat for 11 units. Join two C pieces as shown in Figure 4, referring to Figure 7 for color arrangement; repeat for 12 units.

Figure 2
Sew C to C to B as shown.

Figure 3
Sew B to B as shown.

Figure 4
Join 2 C pieces as shown.

Step 4. Arrange pieced units with A, F and H and join as shown in Figure 5 to make a corner section; repeat for four corner sections, referring to the Placement Diagram and Figure 7 for color arrangement.

Step 5. Arrange pieces and join as shown in Figure 6 to make middle sections; repeat for four middle

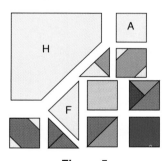

Figure 5
Arrange pieces and join as shown for corner sections.

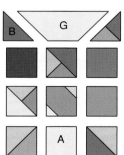

Figure 6
Arrange pieces and join as shown for middle sections.

Autumn Wreath
Placement Diagram
19 1/4" x 29 1/4"

sections, referring to the Placement Diagram and Figure 7 for color arrangement.

Step 6. Join the pieced sections with I to complete Wreath block as shown in Figure 7.

Step 7. Sew two taupe B triangles to J. Sew L to K and KR and sew to the B-J unit. Sew on B to complete one Leaf block as shown in Figure 8.

Step 8. Join three Leaf blocks to make a strip as shown in Figure 9; repeat for second strip. Cut four strips taupe 1" x 4 3/4". Sew a strip to the top and bottom of each leaf strip, again referring to Figure 9; press seams toward strips.

Step 9. Cut two strips gray print 1 1/4" x 14 1/4" for M. Join the leaf strips to opposite sides of the Wreath block with M strips. Cut two more strips gray print 1 1/4" x 24 1/4" for N; sew to top and bottom of pieced section. Cut two more strips gray print 1 1/4" x 15 3/4" for O; sew to opposite sides of pieced section. Press seams toward strips after each addition.

Step 10. Cut two strips burgundy stripe 2 1/2" x 25 3/4" for P; sew to top and bottom of pieced section. Cut two more strips burgundy stripe 2 1/2" x 19 3/4" for Q; sew to remaining sides of pieced section. Press seams toward strips after each addition.

Step 11. Mark the quilting designs given in leaves and on outside borders using a water-erasable pen or marker.

Step 12. Quilt and finish as desired referring to the General Instructions.

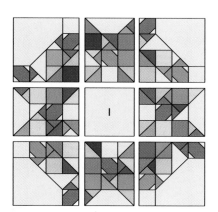

Figure 7
Join pieced sections with I to complete Wreath block.

Figure 8
Join pieces to make Leaf block as shown.

1" X 4 3/4"

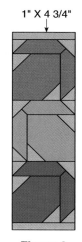

Figure 9
Join Leaf blocks to make strips.

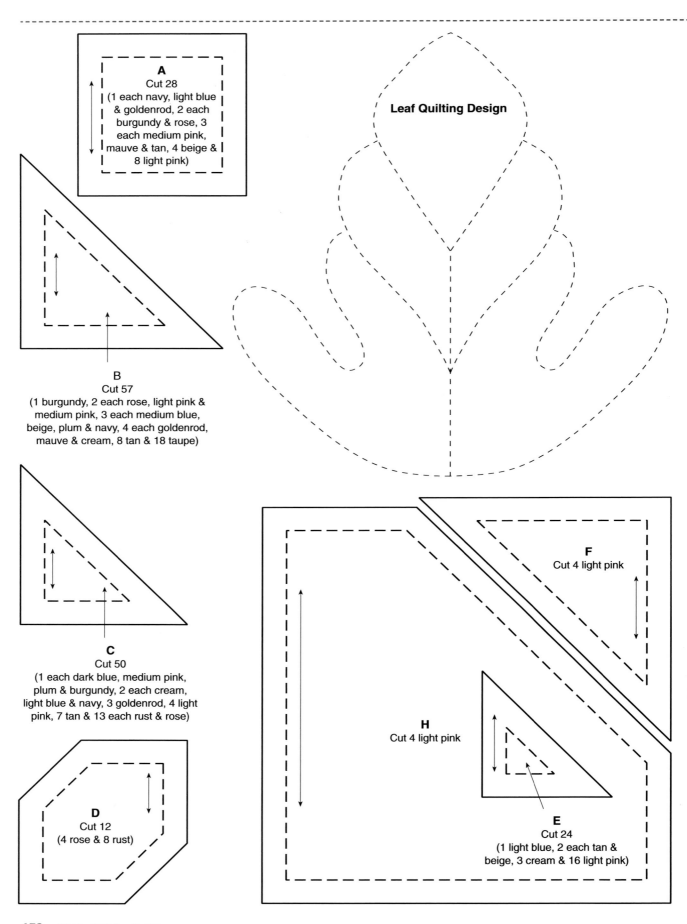

A
Cut 28
(1 each navy, light blue & goldenrod, 2 each burgundy & rose, 3 each medium pink, mauve & tan, 4 beige & 8 light pink)

Leaf Quilting Design

B
Cut 57
(1 burgundy, 2 each rose, light pink & medium pink, 3 each medium blue, beige, plum & navy, 4 each goldenrod, mauve & cream, 8 tan & 18 taupe)

C
Cut 50
(1 each dark blue, medium pink, plum & burgundy, 2 each cream, light blue & navy, 3 goldenrod, 4 light pink, 7 tan & 13 each rust & rose)

D
Cut 12
(4 rose & 8 rust)

F
Cut 4 light pink

H
Cut 4 light pink

E
Cut 24
(1 light blue, 2 each tan & beige, 3 cream & 16 light pink)

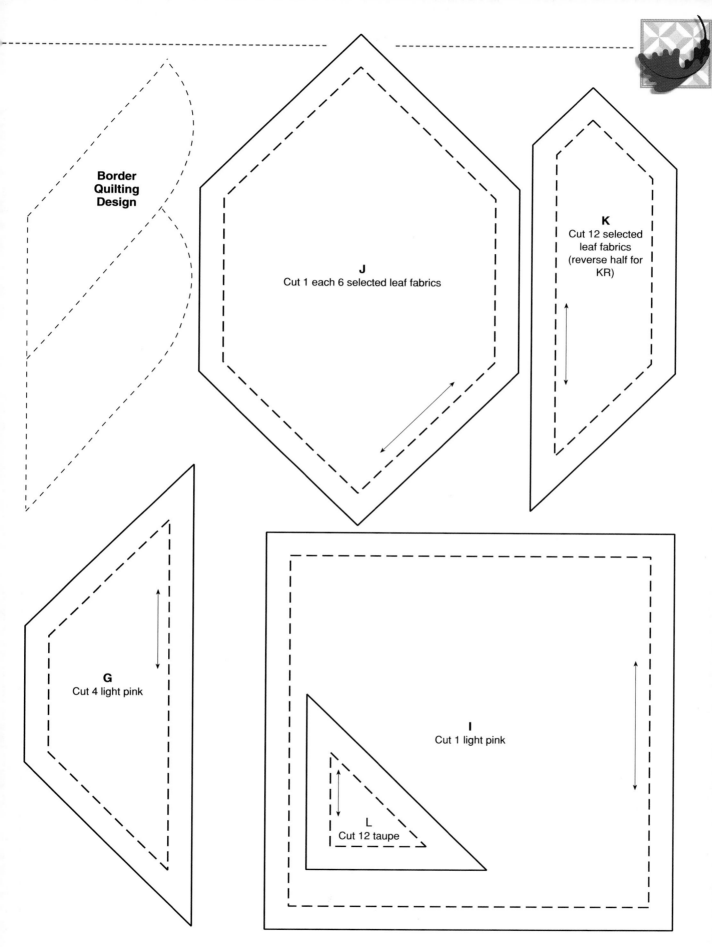

Border Quilting Design

J
Cut 1 each 6 selected leaf fabrics

K
Cut 12 selected leaf fabrics (reverse half for KR)

G
Cut 4 light pink

I
Cut 1 light pink

L
Cut 12 taupe

Pumpkin Delivery

By Lucy A. Fazely

Look for unusual prints to make this Halloween wall quilt. The fabrics used on the sample include owls, cats and owls in trees mixed with spider web prints. Have fun finding seasonal prints to create your own special version!

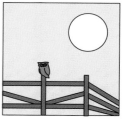

Fence
12" x 12" Block

Tree
12" x 12" Block

Witch
12" x 12" Block

Specifications

Skill Level: Beginner

Quilt Size: 17" x 42"

Block Size: 12" x 12"

Number of Blocks: 3

Materials

3 squares 12 1/2" x 12 1/2" seasonal prints for background blocks

12" x 16" piece brown print for tree, broom and fence

2" x 3" piece orange print for tree's eyes and mouth

6" x 9" piece black print for witch

5" x 5" piece white-and-black print for moon

Scraps novelty prints to add accents of color and design

1/6 yard black print for sashing

1/4 yard orange print for border

12" x 24" fusible transfer web

Cotton batting 20" x 45"

Backing 20" x 45"

3 1/2 yards self-made or purchased Halloween-print binding

Neutral color all-purpose thread

Basic sewing tools and supplies

Instructions

Step 1. Prepare templates for pattern pieces given. Mark the right side of each template.

Step 2. For tree, broom and fence pieces, cut an 11 1/2" x 15 1/2" piece fusible transfer web. Fuse to wrong side of 12" x 16" piece brown print. Lay the tree pattern wrong side down on paper side of fabric; trace shape. Cut out on traced line carefully, including eyes and mouth; remove paper backing. Cut witch's broom and mark center dot; set aside remaining brown print for fence pieces. Cut and remove paper as for tree; set aside.

Step 3. For eyes and mouth shapes, cut a piece of fusible transfer web 1 1/2" x 2 1/2"; fuse to wrong side of 2" x 3" piece of orange print. Trace eyes and mouth shapes onto paper side of fabric. Cut out on traced lines; remove paper backing.

Step 4. Center tree on bottom center of one background square referring to the Placement Diagram for positioning. Place eyes and mouth under cutout openings; fuse shapes in place following manufacturer's instructions.

Step 5. For witch, cut a piece of fusible transfer web 5 1/2" x 8 1/2"; fuse to wrong side of 6" x 9" piece black print. Place the witch pattern on paper side of black print wrong side down; trace. Cut out shape and mark center dot; remove paper backing.

Step 6. For placement of broom, line up dots marked on broom and witch shapes. Center witch and broom with witch on top on a 12 1/2" x 12 1/2" background square referring to the Placement Diagram; fuse in place.

Step 7. For fence pieces, cut 11 segments each 1/2" x 4" fused brown print. Remove paper backing and lay out fence pieces on remaining 12 1/2" x 12 1/2" background square referring to the Placement Diagram and photo of project for positioning suggestions; fuse in place.

Step 8. For moon, cut a 4 1/2" x 4 1/2" piece fusible transfer web; fuse to wrong side of 5" x 5" square white-and-black print. Trace a 4"-diameter circle on the paper side of fabric. Cut out; remove paper backing.

Step 9. Position moon circle 1 1/4" from top and 1 1/2" in from right side of the fence block referring to Placement Diagram; fuse in place.

Step 10. Add accents such as the owls on the fence and tree and pumpkin on broom from novelty prints. To use, cut shape from fabric, leaving excess all around. Cut a piece of fusible transfer web a bit smaller than the cut-out section; fuse to wrong side of piece. Cut out shape around edges; remove paper backing. Position shapes as desired; fuse in place.

Step 11. Cut four strips black print sashing fabric 1" x 12 1/2". Sew blocks together with strips, beginning and ending with a strip; press seams toward strips.

Step 12. From black print, cut two strips 1" x 38 1/2"; sew to top and bottom. Press seams toward strips.

Step 13. Cut two strips orange print 2 1/2" x 38 1/2"; sew to top and bottom. Cut two more strips orange print 2 1/2" x 17 1/2"; sew a strip to opposite ends. Press all seams toward strips.

Step 14. Finish referring to General Instructions.

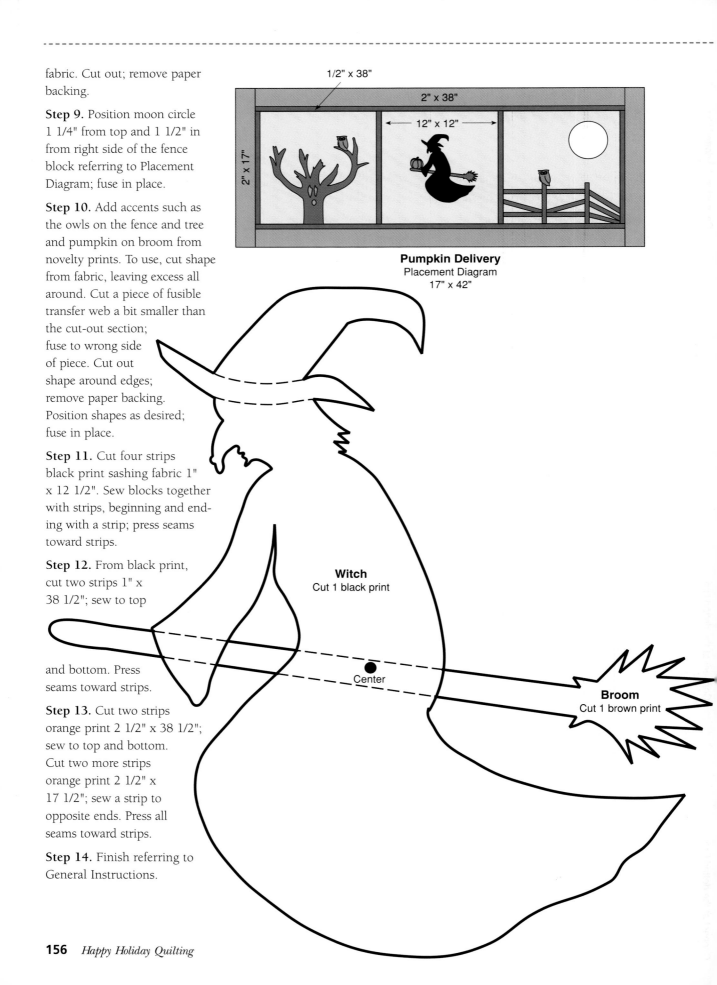

Pumpkin Delivery
Placement Diagram
17" x 42"

Witch
Cut 1 black print

Center

Broom
Cut 1 brown print

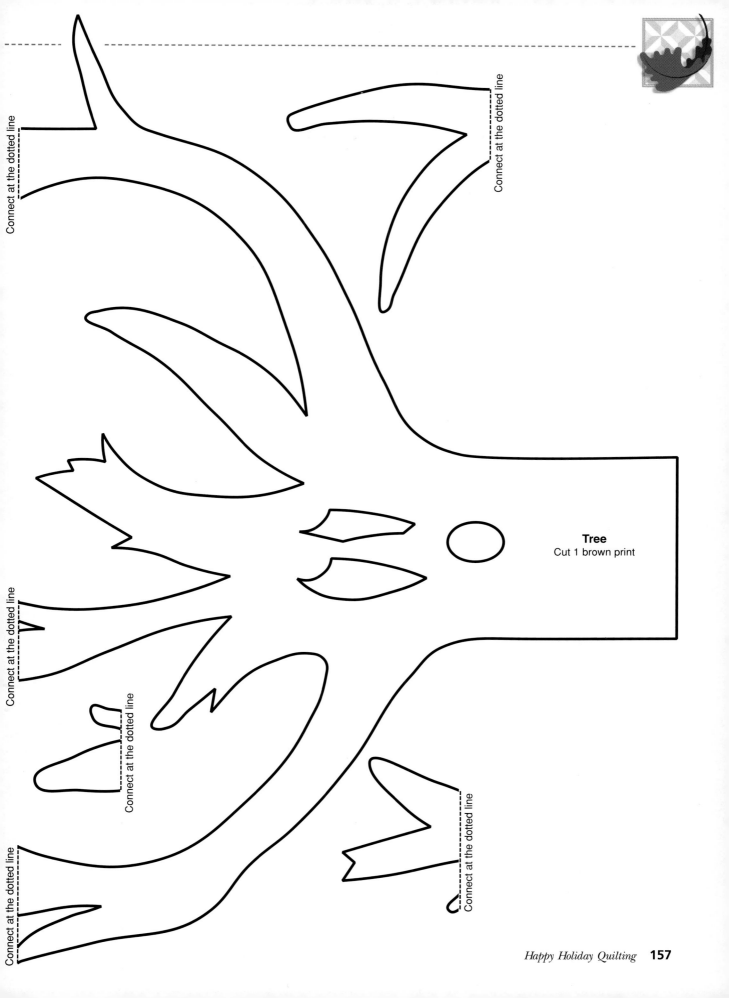

Connect at the dotted line

Connect at the dotted line

Connect at the dotted line

Connect at the dotted line

Connect at the dotted line

Connect at the dotted line

Tree
Cut 1 brown print

Thanksgiving

By Connie Rand

Thanksgiving is a time to thank God for the blessings in our lives. Make this pretty table cover using a harvest print to share your love of quilting during your family gathering.

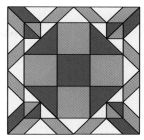

Thanksgiving
16" x 16" Block

Specifications

Skill Level: Advanced Beginner

Quilt Size: 64" x 80"

Block Size: 16" x 16"

Number of Blocks: 20

Materials

2 3/4 yards Thanksgiving print

1 3/4 yards cream-on-cream print

1 3/4 yards dark green solid

Batting 68" x 84"

Backing 68" x 84"

Neutral color all-purpose thread

8 1/2 yards self-made or purchased binding

Basic sewing tools and supplies

Piecing Blocks

Step 1. Prepare templates using pattern pieces given. Cut as directed on each piece for one block; repeat for 20 blocks.

Step 2. Referring to Figure 1, sew a dark green A square between two Thanksgiving print A squares. Sew a dark green C to a Thanksgiving print C. Sew a cream-on-cream print C to each side. Repeat for four C units.

Step 3. Sew the C unit to B. Repeat for four B-C units. Sew a Thanksgiving print A between two B-C units. Repeat.

Step 4. Sew the A unit made in Step 2 between two B-C units made in Step 3 to make the center of the block.

Step 5. Sew a green DR to E to a

Thanksgiving
Placement Diagram
64" x 80"

Thanksgiving print D to E to a Thanksgiving print DR to E to a Thanksgiving print D to make side units; repeat for four units. Sew side units to pieced center to complete block; repeat for 20 blocks.

Step 6. Sew blocks together in five rows of four blocks each, referring to the Placement Diagram.

Step 7. Prepare quilt for quilting and finish referring to General Instructions.

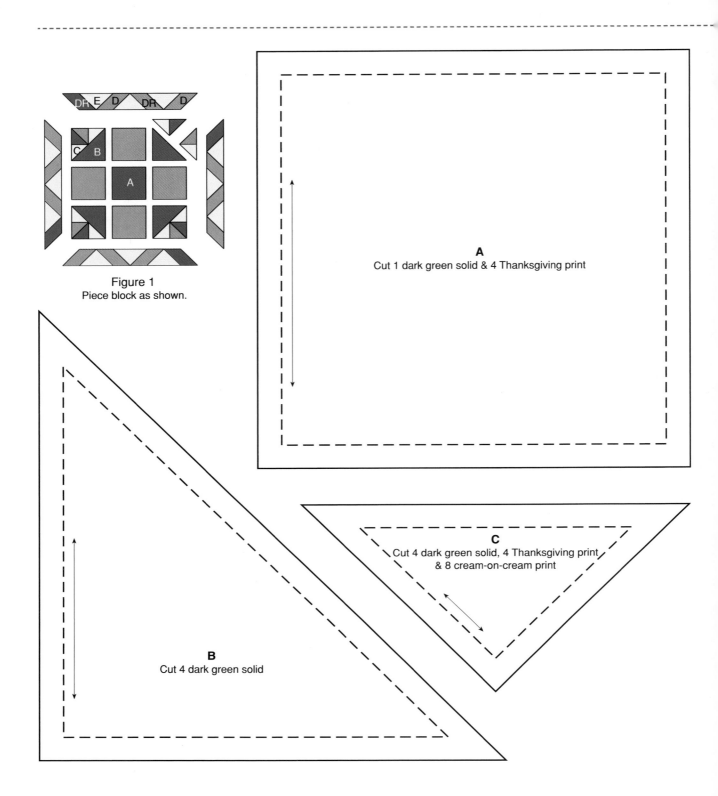

Figure 1
Piece block as shown.

A
Cut 1 dark green solid & 4 Thanksgiving print

B
Cut 4 dark green solid

C
Cut 4 dark green solid, 4 Thanksgiving print
& 8 cream-on-cream print

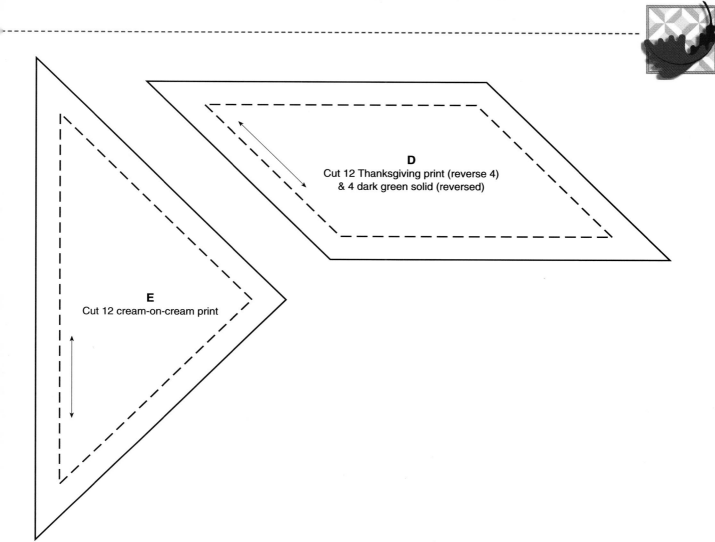

D
Cut 12 Thanksgiving print (reverse 4)
& 4 dark green solid (reversed)

E
Cut 12 cream-on-cream print

Family Tree Anniversary Quilt
Continued from page 145

threads tightly at back of quilt. Repeat for number of buttons needed for photos.

Step 4. Decorate remainder of tree with pearls, beads, charms, etc, stitching each one through to the backside of the quilt to hold layers together.

Step 5. Bind the ends of the gold cord tightly with gold metallic floss to prevent raveling. Fasten the cord all around with thread or glue next to the border seams, butting the ends at the lower center.

Step 6. Tie a bow using gold ribbon. Tack or glue to cover ends of cord.

Making a Legend

A legend should be attached to the back of this project stating who it was made for, the occasion and date, by whom, the relationship of each person in the photos and any other pertinent information.

To make a legend, use a fine-tip permanent fabric marker or pen and a square of muslin. Other methods may be used but they require special computer and printer equipment.

If you like to embroider, hand-stitch the legend onto fabric, then attach the fabric to the back of the quilt.

Make a larger tree if you want to add more people to the tree than space permits at this size.

General Instructions

Quiltmaking Basics
Materials & Supplies

FABRICS

Fabric Choices. Scrap quilts combine fabrics of many types, depending on the quilt. Antique crazy quilts combined silk, wool and cotton. This combination requires special care and use because some fabrics are more fragile than others. It is best to combine same-fiber-content fabrics when making scrap quilts.

Buying Fabrics. One hundred percent cotton fabrics are recommended for making quilts. Choose colors similar to those used in the quilts shown or colors of your own preference. Most scrap quilt designs depend more on contrast of values than on the colors used to create the design.

Preparing the Fabric for Use. Fabrics may be prewashed depending on your preference. Whether you prewash or not, be sure your fabrics are color-fast and won't run onto each other when washed after use.

Fabric Grain. Fabrics are woven with threads going in a crosswise and lengthwise direction. The threads cross at right angles—the more threads per inch, the stronger the fabric.

The crosswise threads will stretch a little. The lengthwise threads will not stretch at all. Cutting the fabric at a 45-degree angle to the crosswise and lengthwise threads produces a bias edge which stretches a great deal when pulled (Figure 1).

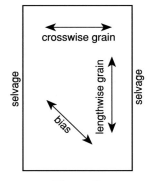

Figure 1
Drawing shows lengthwise, crosswise and bias threads.

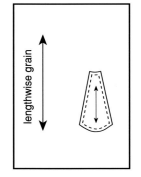

Figure 2
Place the template with marked arrow on the lengthwise grain of the fabric.

If templates are given with patterns in this book, pay careful attention to the grain lines marked with arrows. These arrows indicate that the piece should be placed on the lengthwise grain with the arrow running on one thread. Although it is not necessary to examine the fabric and find a thread to match to, it is important to try to place the arrow with the lengthwise grain of the fabric (Figure 2).

THREAD

For most piecing, good-quality cotton or cotton-covered polyester is the thread of choice. Inexpensive polyester threads are not recommended because they can cut the fibers of cotton fabrics.

Choose a color thread that will match or blend with the fabrics in your quilt. Most scrap quilts are pieced with dark and light color fabrics. Choose a neutral thread color, such as a medium gray, as a compromise between colors. Test by pulling a sample seam.

BATTING

Batting is the material used to give a quilt loft or thickness. It also adds warmth.

Batting size is listed in inches for each pattern to reflect the size needed to complete the quilt according to the instructions. Purchase the size large enough to cut the size you need for the quilt of your choice.

Some qualities to look for in batting are drapability, resistance to fiber migration, loft and softness.

If you are unsure which kind of batting to use, purchase the smallest size batting available in the type you'd like to try. Test each sample on a small project. Choose the batting that you like working with most and that will result in the type of quilt you need.

TOOLS & EQUIPMENT

There are few truly essential tools and little equipment required for quiltmaking. Basics include needles (hand-sewing and quilting betweens), pins (long, thin sharp pins are best), sharp scissors or shears, a thimble, template materials (plastic or cardboard), marking tools (chalk marker, water-erasable pen and a No. 2 pencil are a few) and a quilting frame or hoop. For piecing and/or quilting by machine, add a sewing machine to the list.

Other sewing basics such as a seam ripper, pincushion, measuring tape and an iron are also necessary. For choosing colors or quilting designs for your quilt, or for designing your own quilt, it is helpful to have on hand graph paper, tracing paper, colored pencils or markers and a ruler.

For making scrap quilts, a rotary cutter, mat and specialty rulers are often used. We recommend an ergonomic rotary cutter, a large self-healing mat and several rulers. If you can choose only one size, a 6" x 24" marked in 1/8" or 1/4" increments is recommended.

Construction Methods

Traditional Templates. While some quilt instructions in this book use rotary-cut strips and quick sewing methods, many patterns require a template. Templates are like the pattern pieces used to sew a garment. They are used to cut the fabric pieces which make up the quilt top. There are two types—templates that include a 1/4" seam allowance and those that don't.

Choose the template material and the pattern. Transfer the pattern shapes to the template material with a sharp No. 2 lead pencil. Write the pattern name, piece letter or number, grain line and number to cut for one block or whole quilt on each piece as shown in Figure 3.

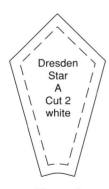

Figure 3
Mark each template with the pattern
name and piece identification.

Some patterns require a reversed piece (Figure 4). These patterns are labeled with an R after the piece letter; for example, B and BR. To reverse a template, first cut it with the labeled side up and then with the labeled side down. Compare these to the right and left fronts of a blouse. When making a garment, you accomplish reversed pieces when cutting the pattern on two layers of

fabric placed with right sides together. This can be done when cutting templates as well.

If cutting one layer of fabric at a time, first trace the template onto the backside of the fabric with the marked side down; turn the template over with the marked side up to make reverse pieces.

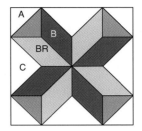

Figure 4
This pattern uses reversed pieces.

Hand-Piecing Basics. When hand-piecing it is easier to begin with templates which do not include the 1/4" seam allowance. Place the template on the wrong side of the fabric, lining up the marked grain line with lengthwise or crosswise fabric grain. If the piece does not have to be reversed, place with labeled side up. Trace around shape; move, leaving 1/2" between the shapes, and mark again.

When you have marked the appropriate number of pieces, cut out pieces, leaving 1/4" beyond marked line all around each piece.

Patterns in this book include a drawing suggesting the assembly order. Refer to these drawings to piece units and blocks.

To join two units, place the patches with right sides together. Stick a pin in at the beginning of the seam through both fabric patches, matching the beginning points (Figure 5); for hand-piecing, the seam begins on the traced line, not at the edge of the fabric (see Figure 6).

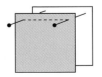

Figure 5
Stick a pin through
fabrics to match the
beginning of the seam.

Figure 6
Begin hand-piecing at seam,
not at the edge of the fabric.
Continue stitching along
seam line.

Thread a sharp needle; knot one strand of the thread at the end. Remove the pin and insert the needle in the hole; make a short stitch and then a backstitch right over the first stitch. Continue making short stitches with several stitches on the needle at one time. As you stitch, check the back piece often to assure accurate stitching on the seam line. Take a stitch at the end of the seam; backstitch and knot at the same time as shown in Figure 7.

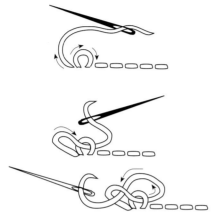

Figure 7
Make a loop in a backstitch to make a knot.

Seams on hand-pieced fabric patches may be finger-pressed toward the darker fabric.

To sew units together, pin fabric patches together, matching seams. Sew as above except where seams meet; at these intersections, backstitch, go through seam to next piece and backstitch again to secure seam joint.

Not all pieced blocks can be stitched with straight seams or in rows. Some patterns require set-in pieces. To begin a set-in seam, pin one side of the square to the proper side of the star point with right sides together, matching corners. Start stitching at the seam line on the outside point; stitch on the marked seam line to the end of the seam line at the center referring to Figure 8.

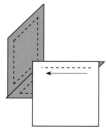

Figure 8
To set a square into a diamond point, match seams and stitch from outside edge to center.

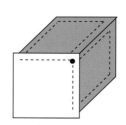

Figure 9
Continue stitching the adjacent side of the square to the next diamond shape in 1 seam from center to outside as shown.

Bring around the adjacent side and pin to the next star point, matching seams. Continue the stitching line from the adjacent seam through corners and to the outside edge of the square as shown in Figure 9.

Machine-Piecing. If making templates, include the 1/4" seam allowance on the template for machine-piecing. Place template on the wrong side of the fabric as for hand-piecing except butt pieces against one another when tracing.

Set machine on 2.5 or 12–15 stitches per inch. Join pieces as for hand-piecing for set-in seams; but for other straight seams, begin and end sewing at the end of the fabric patch sewn as shown in Figure 10. No backstitching is necessary when machine-stitching.

Join units as for hand-piecing referring to the piecing diagrams where needed. Chain piecing (Figure 11—sewing several like units before sewing other units) saves time by eliminating beginning and ending stitches.

When joining machine-pieced units, match seams against each other with seam allowances pressed in opposite directions to reduce bulk and make perfect matching of seams possible (Figure 12).

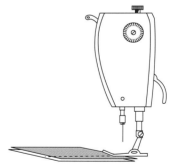

Figure 10
Begin machine-piecing at the end of the piece, not at the end of the seam.

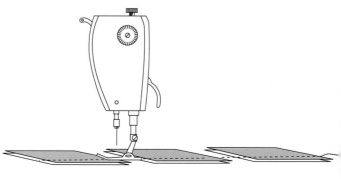

Figure 11
Units may be chain-pieced to save time.

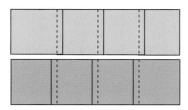

Figure 12
Sew machine-pieced units with seams
pressed in opposite directions.

Quick-Cutting. Quick-cutting and piecing strips is recommended for making many of the scrap quilts in this book. Templates are completely eliminated; instead, a rotary cutter, plastic ruler and mat are used to cut fabric strips.

When rotary-cutting strips, straighten raw edges of fabric by folding fabric in fourths across the width as shown in Figure 13. Press down flat; place ruler on fabric square with edge of fabric and make one cut from the folded edge to the outside edge. If strips are not straightened, a wavy strip will result as shown in Figure 14.

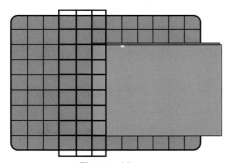

Figure 13
Fold fabric and straighten as shown.

Figure 14
Wavy strips result if fabric is not straightened before cutting.

Always cut away from your body, holding the ruler firmly with the non-cutting hand. Keep fingers away from the edge of the ruler as it is easy for the rotary cutter to slip and jump over the edge of the ruler if cutting is not properly done.

If a square is required for the pattern, it can be sub-cut from a strip as shown in Figure 15.

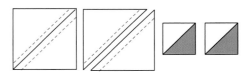

Figure 15
If cutting squares, cut proper-width strip into same-width segments. Here, a 2" strip is cut into 2" segments to create 2" squares. These squares finish at 1 1/2" when sewn.

If you need right triangles with the straight grain on the short sides, you can use the same method, but you need to figure out how wide to cut the strip. Measure the finished size of one short side of the triangle. Add 7/8" to this size for seam allowance. Cut fabric strips this width; cut the strips into the same increment to create squares. Cut the squares on the diagonal to produce triangles. For example, if you need a triangle with a 2" finished height, cut the strips 2 7/8" by the width of the fabric. Cut the strips into 2 7/8" squares. Cut each square on the diagonal to produce the correct-size triangle with the grain on the short sides (Figure 16).

Triangles sewn together to make squares are called half-square triangles or triangle/squares. When joined, the triangle/square unit has the straight of grain on all outside edges of the block.

Another method of making triangle/squares is shown in Figure 17. Layer two squares with right sides together; draw a diagonal line through the center. Stitch 1/4" on both sides of the line. Cut apart on the drawn line to reveal two stitched triangle/squares.

If you need triangles with the straight of grain on the diagonal, such as for fill-in triangles on the outside edges of a diagonal-set quilt, the procedure is a bit different.

To make these triangles, a square is cut on both diagonals; thus, the straight of grain is on the longest or diagonal side (Figure 18). To figure out the size to cut the square, add 1 1/4" to the needed finished size of the longest side of the triangle. For example, if you need a triangle with a 12" finished diagonal, cut a 13 1/4" square.

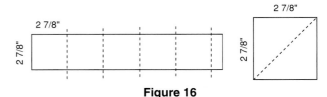

Figure 16
Cut 2" (finished size) triangles from 2 7/8" squares as shown.

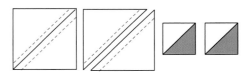

Figure 17
Mark a diagonal line on the square; stitch
1/4" on each side of the line. Cut on line
to reveal stitched triangle/squares.

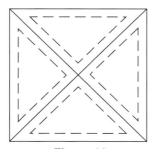

Figure 18
Add 1 1/4" to the finished size of the
longest side of the triangle needed
and cut on both diagonals to make a
quarter-square triangle.

If templates are given, use their measurments to cut fabric strips to correspond with that measurement. The template may be used on the strip to cut pieces quickly. Strip cutting works best for squares, triangles, rectangles and diamonds. Odd-shaped templates are difficult to cut in multiple layers or using a rotary cutter.

Quick-Piecing Method. Lay pieces to be joined under the presser foot of the sewing machine right sides together. Sew an exact 1/4" seam allowance to the end of the piece; place another unit right next to the first one and continue sewing, adding a piece after every stitched piece, until all of the pieces are used up (Figure 19).

When sewing is finished, cut threads joining the pieces apart. Press seam toward the darker fabric.

Figure 19
Sew pieces together in a chain.

Foundation Piecing. Paper or fabric foundation pieces are used to make very accurate blocks, provide stability for weak fabrics, and add body and weight to the finished quilt.

Temporary foundation materials include paper, tracing paper, freezer paper and removable interfacing. Permanent foundations include utility fabrics, non-woven interfacing, flannel, fleece and batting.

Methods of marking foundations include basting lines, pencils or pens, needlepunching, tracing wheel, hot-iron transfers, copy machine, pre-marked, stamps or stencils.

There are two methods of foundation piecing—under-piecing and top-piecing. When under-piecing, the pattern is reversed when tracing. We have not included any patterns for top-piecing.

Note: All patterns for which we recommend paper piecing are already reversed in full-size drawings given.

To under-piece, place a scrap of fabric larger than the lined space on the unlined side of the paper in the No. 1 position. Place piece 2 right sides together with piece 1; pin on seam line, and fold back to check that the piece will cover space 2 before stitching.

Stitch along line on the lined side of the paper—fabric will not be visible. Sew several stitches beyond the beginning and ending of the line. Backstitching is not required as another fabric seam will cover this seam.

Remove pin; finger-press piece 2 flat. Continue adding all pieces in numerical order in the same manner until all pieces are stitched to paper. Trim excess to outside line (1/4" larger all around than finished size of the block).

Tips & Techniques

If you cannot see the lines on the backside of the paper when paper-piecing, draw over lines with a small felt-tip marker. The lines should now be visible on the backside to help with placement of fabric pieces.

Before machine-piecing fabric patches together, test your sewing machine for positioning an accurate 1/4" seam allowance. There are several tools to help guarantee this. Some machine needles may be moved to allow the presser-foot edge to be a 1/4" guide.

A special foot may be purchased for your machine that will guarantee an accurate 1/4" seam. A piece of masking tape can be placed on the throat plate of your sewing machine to mark the 1/4" seam. A plastic stick-on ruler may be used instead of tape with the same results.

Tracing paper can be used as a temporary foundation. It is removed when blocks are complete and stitched together. To paper-piece, copy patterns given here using a copy machine or trace each block individually. Measure the finished paper foundations to insure accuracy in copying.

Putting It All Together

Many steps are required to prepare a quilt top for quilting, including setting the blocks together, adding borders, choosing and marking quilting designs, layering the top, batting and backing for quilting, quilting or tying the layers and finishing the edges of the quilt.

As you begin the process of finishing your quilt top, strive for a neat, flat quilt with square sides and corners, not for perfection—that will come with time and practice.

Finishing the Top

Settings. Most quilts are made by sewing individual blocks together in rows which, when joined, create a design. There are several other methods used to join blocks. Sometimes the setting choice is determined by the block's design. For example, a house block should be placed upright on a quilt, not sideways or upside down.

Plain blocks can be alternated with pieced or appliquéd blocks in a straight set. Making a quilt using plain blocks saves time; half the number of pieced or appliquéd blocks are needed to make the same-size quilt as shown in Figure 1.

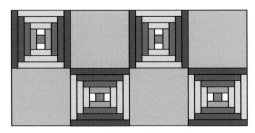

Figure 1
Alternate plain blocks with pieced blocks to save time.

Adding Borders. Borders are an integral part of the quilt and should complement the colors and designs used in the quilt center. Borders frame a quilt just like a mat and frame do a picture.

If fabric strips are added for borders, they may be mitered or butted at the corners as shown in

Figures 2 and 3. To determine the size for butted border strips, measure across the center of the completed quilt top from one side raw edge to the other side raw edge. This measurement will include a 1/4" seam allowance.

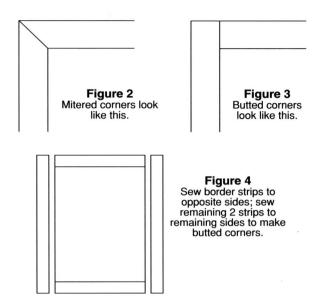

Figure 2
Mitered corners look like this.

Figure 3
Butted corners look like this.

Figure 4
Sew border strips to opposite sides; sew remaining 2 strips to remaining sides to make butted corners.

Cut two border strips that length by the chosen width of the border. Sew these strips to the top and bottom of the pieced center referring to Figure 4. Press the seam allowance toward the border strips.

Measure across the completed quilt top at the center, from top raw edge to bottom raw edge, including the two border strips already added. Cut two border strips that length by the chosen width of the border. Sew a strip to each of the two remaining sides as shown in Figure 4. Press the seams toward the border strips.

To make mitered corners, measure the quilt as before. To this add twice the width of the border and 1/2" for seam allowances to determine the length of the strips. Repeat for opposite sides. Sew on each strip, stopping stitching 1/4" from corner, leaving the remainder of the strip dangling.

Press corners at a 45-degree angle to form a crease. Stitch from the inside quilt corner to the outside on the creased line. Trim excess away after stitching and press mitered seams open (Figures 5–7).

Carefully press the entire piece, including the pieced center. Avoid pulling and stretching while pressing, which would distort shapes.

Figure 5
For mitered corner, stitch strip,
stopping 1/4" from corner seam.

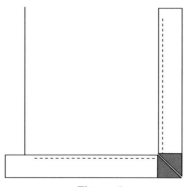

Figure 6
Fold and press corner to make a
45-degree angle.

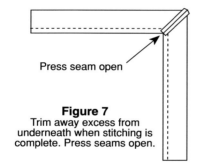

Press seam open

Figure 7
Trim away excess from
underneath when stitching is
complete. Press seams open.

Getting Ready to Quilt

Choosing a Quilting Design. If you choose to hand- or machine-quilt your finished top, you will need to choose a design for quilting.

There are several types of quilting designs, some of which may not have to be marked. The easiest of the unmarked designs is in-the-ditch quilting. Here the quilting stitches are placed in the valley created by the seams joining two pieces together or next to the edge of an appliqué design. There is no need to mark a top for in-the-ditch quilting. Machine quilters choose this option because the stitches are not as obvious on the finished quilt. (Figure 8).

Outline-quilting 1/4" or more away from seams or appliqué shapes is another no-mark alternative

(Figure 9) which prevents having to sew through the layers made by seams, thus making stitching easier.

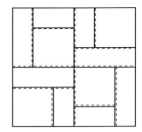

Figure 8
In-the-ditch quilting is done in
the seam that joins 2 pieces.

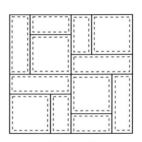

Figure 9
Outline-quilting 1/4" away
from seam is a popular
choice for quilting.

If you are not comfortable eyeballing the 1/4" (or other distance), masking tape is available in different widths and is helpful to place on straight-edge designs to mark the quilting line. If using masking tape, place the tape right up against the seam and quilt close to the other edge.

Meander or free-motion quilting by machine fills in open spaces and doesn't require marking. It is fun and easy to stitch as shown in Figure 10.

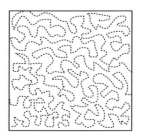

Figure 10
Machine meander quilting
fills in large spaces.

Marking the Top for Quilting or Tying. If you choose a fancy or allover design for quilting, you will need to transfer the design to your quilt top before layering with the backing and batting. You may use a sharp medium-lead or silver pencil on light background fabrics. Wash-out markers and chalk may also be used. Test the pencil marks to guarantee that they will wash out of your quilt top when quilting is complete; or be sure your quilting stitches cover the pencil marks. Mechanical pencils with very fine points may be used successfully to mark quilts.

Manufactured quilt-design templates are available in many designs and sizes and are cut out of a durable plastic template material which is easy to use.

To make a permanent quilt-design template, choose a template material on which to transfer the design. See-through plastic is the best as it will let you place the design while allowing you to see where it is in relation to your quilt design without moving it. Place the design on the quilt top where you want it and trace around it with your marking tool. Pick up the quilting template and place again; repeat marking.

No matter what marking method you use, remember—the marked lines should *never show* on the finished quilt. When the top is marked, it is ready for layering.

Preparing the Quilt Backing. The quilt backing is a very important feature of your quilt. In most cases, the Materials list for each quilt in this book gives the size requirements for the backing, not the yardage needed. Exceptions to this are when the backing fabric is also used on the quilt top and yardage is given for that fabric.

A backing is generally cut at least 4" larger than the quilt top or 2" larger on all sides. For a 64" x 78" finished quilt, the backing would need to be at least 68" x 82".

To avoid having the seam across the center of the quilt backing, cut or tear one of the right-length pieces in half and sew half to each side of the second piece as shown in Figure 11.

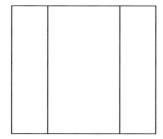

Figure 11
Center 1 backing piece with a piece on each side.

Quilts that need a backing more than 88" wide may be pieced in horizontal pieces as shown in Figure 12.

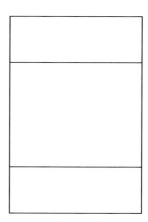

Figure 12
Horizontal seams may be used on backing pieces.

Layering the Quilt Sandwich. Layering the quilt top with the batting and backing is time-consuming. Open the batting several days before you need it and place over a bed or flat on the floor to help flatten the creases caused from being folded in the bag for so long.

Iron the backing piece, folding in half both vertically and horizontally and pressing to mark centers.

If you will not be quilting on a frame, place the backing right side down on a clean floor or table. Start in the center and push any wrinkles or bunches flat. Use masking tape to tape the edges to the floor or large clips to hold the backing to the edges of the table. The backing should be taut.

Place the batting on top of the backing, matching centers using fold lines as guides; flatten out any wrinkles. Trim the batting to the same size as the backing.

Fold the quilt top in half lengthwise and place on top of the batting, wrong side against the batting, matching centers. Unfold quilt and, working from the center to the outside edges, smooth out any wrinkles or lumps.

To hold the quilt layers together for quilting, baste by hand or use safety pins. If basting by hand, thread a long thin needle with a long piece of unknotted white or off-white thread. Starting in the center and leaving a long tail, make 4"–6" stitches toward the outside edge of the quilt top, smoothing as you baste. Start at the center again and work toward the outside as shown in Figure 13.

If quilting by machine, you may prefer to use safety pins for holding your fabric sandwich together. Start in the center of the quilt and pin to the outside, leaving pins open until all are placed.

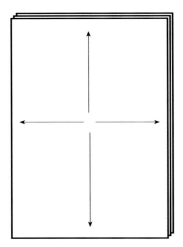

Figure 13
Baste from the center to the outside edges.

When you are satisfied that all layers are smooth, close the pins.

QUILTING

Hand Quilting. Hand quilting is the process of placing stitches through the quilt top, batting and backing to hold them together. While it is a functional process, it also adds beauty and loft to the finished quilt.

To begin, thread a sharp between needle with an 18" piece of quilting thread. Tie a small knot in the end of the thread. Position the needle about 1/2" to 1" away from the starting point on quilt top. Sink the needle through the top into the batting layer but not through the backing. Pull the needle up at the starting point of the quilting design. Pull the needle and thread until the knot sinks through the top into the batting (Figure 14).

Some stitchers like to take a backstitch here at the beginning while others prefer to begin the first

Figure 14
Start the needle through the top layer of fabric 1/2"–1" away from quilting line with knot on top of fabric.

stitch. Take small, even running stitches along the marked quilting line (Figure 15). Keep one hand positioned underneath to feel the needle go all the way through to the backing.

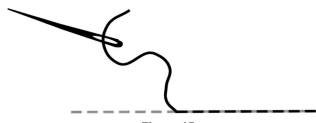

Figure 15
Make small, even running stitches on marked quilting line.

Machine Quilting. Successful machine quilting requires practice and a good relationship with your sewing machine.

Prepare the quilt for machine quilting in the same way as for hand-quilting. Use safety pins to hold the layers together instead of basting with thread.

Presser-foot quilting is best used for straight-line quilting because the presser bar lever does not need to be continually lifted.

Set the machine on a longer stitch length (3.0 or 8–10 stitches to the inch). Too tight a stitch causes puckering and fabric tucks, either on the quilt top

Protect Your Fingers

Use a thimble to prevent sore fingers when hand quilting. The finger that is under the quilt to feel the needle as it passes through the backing is the one that is most apt to get sore from the pin pricks. Some quilters purchase leather thimbles for this finger while others try home remedies. One simple aid is masking tape wrapped around the finger. With the tape you will still be able to feel the needle, but it will not prick your skin.

Over time calluses build up and these fingers get toughened up, but with every vacation from quilting, they will become soft and the process begins again.

or backing. An even-feed or walking foot helps to eliminate the tucks and puckering by feeding the upper and lower layers through the machine evenly. Before you begin, loosen the amount of pressure on the presser foot.

Special machine-quilting needles work best to penetrate the three layers in your quilt. Decide on a design. Quilting in the ditch is not quite as visible, but if you quilt with the feed dogs engaged, it means turning the quilt frequently. It is not easy to fit a rolled-up quilt through the small opening on the sewing machine head.

Meander quilting is the easiest way to machine-quilt—and it is fun. Meander quilting is done using an appliqué or darning foot with the feed dogs dropped. It is sort of like scribbling. Simply move the quilt top around under the foot and make stitches in a random pattern to fill the space. The same method may be used to outline a quilt design.

The trick is the same as in hand-quilting; you are striving for stitches of uniform size. Your hands are in complete control of the design.

If machine-quilting is of interest to you, there are several very good books available at quilt shops that will help you become a successful machine quilter.

Tied Quilts, or Comforters. Would you rather tie your quilt layers together than quilt them? Tied quilts are often referred to as comforters. The advantage of tying is that it takes so much less time and the required skills can be learned quickly.

If a top will be tied, choose a thick, bonded batting—one that will not separate during washing. For tying, use pearl cotton, embroidery floss, or strong yarn in colors that match or coordinate with the fabrics in your quilt top.

Decide on a pattern for tying. Many quilts are tied at the corners and centers of the blocks and at sashing joints. Try to tie every 4"–6". Special designs can be used for tying, but most quilts are tied in conventional ways. Begin tying in the center and work to the outside edges.

To make the tie, thread a large needle with a long thread (yarn, floss or crochet cotton); do not knot. Push the needle through the quilt top to the back, leaving a 3"–4" length on top. Move the needle to the next position without cutting thread. Take another stitch through the layers; repeat until thread is almost used up.

Cut thread between stitches, leaving an equal amount of thread on each stitch. Tie a knot with

the two thread ends. Tie again to make a square knot referring to Figure 16. Trim thread ends to desired length.

Figure 16
Make a square knot as shown.

Hand-Quilting Hints

Knots should not show on the quilt top or back. Learn to sink the knot into the batting at the beginning and ending of the quilting thread for successful stitches. Making 12–18 stitches per inch is a nice goal, but a more realistic goal is seven to nine stitches per inch. If you cannot accomplish this right away, strive for even stitches—all the same size—that look as good on the back as on the front.

When you have nearly run out of thread, wind the thread around the needle several times to make a small knot and pull it close to the fabric. Insert the needle into the fabric on the quilting line and come out with the needle 1/2" to 1" away, pulling the knot into the fabric layers the same as when you started. Pull and cut thread close to fabric. The end should disappear inside after cutting. Some quilters prefer to take a backstitch with a loop through it for a knot to end.

You will perfect your quilting stitches as you gain experience, your stitches will get better with each project and your style will be uniquely your own.

Finishing the Edges

After your quilt is tied or quilted, the edges need to be finished. Decide how you want the edges of your quilt finished before layering the backing and batting with the quilt top.

Without Binding—Self-Finish. There is one way to eliminate adding an edge finish. This is done before quilting. Place the batting on a flat surface. Place the pieced top right side up on the batting. Place the backing right sides together with the pieced top. Pin and/or baste the layers together to hold flat.

Begin stitching in the center of one side using a 1/4" seam allowance, reversing at the beginning and end of the seam. Continue stitching all around and back to the beginning side. Leave a 12" or larger opening. Clip corners and trim seams to reduce excess. Turn right side out through the opening. Slipstitch the opening closed by hand. The quilt may now be quilted by hand or machine.

The disadvantage to this method is that once the edges are sewn in, any creases or wrinkles that might form during the quilting process cannot be flattened out. Tying is the preferred method for finishing a quilt constructed using this method.

Bringing the backing fabric to the front is another way to finish the quilt's edge without binding. To accomplish this, complete the quilt as for hand or machine quilting. Trim the batting *only* even with the front. Trim the backing 1" larger than the completed top all around.

Turn the backing edge in 1/2" and then turn over to the front along edge of batting. The folded edge may be machine-stitched close to the edge through all layers, or blind-stitched in place to finish.

The front may be turned to the back. If using this method, a wider front border is needed. The backing and batting are trimmed 1" *smaller* than the top and the top edge is turned under 1/2" and then turned to the back and stitched in place.

One more method of self-finish may be used. The top and backing may be stitched together by hand at the edge. To accomplish this, all quilting must be stopped 1/2" from the quilt-top edge. The top and backing of the quilt are trimmed even and the batting is trimmed to 1/4"–1/2" smaller. The edges of the top and backing are turned in 1/4"–1/2" and blind-stitched together at the very edge.

These methods do not require the use of extra fabric and save time in preparation of binding strips; they are not as durable as an added binding.

Binding. The technique of adding extra fabric at the edges of the quilt is called binding. The binding encloses the edges and adds an extra layer of fabric for durability.

To prepare the quilt for the addition of the binding, trim the batting and backing layers flush with the top of the quilt using a rotary cutter and ruler or shears. Using a walking-foot attachment (sometimes called an even-feed foot attachment), machine-baste the three layers together all around approximately 1/8" from the cut edge.

The list of materials given with each quilt in this book often includes a number of yards of self-made or purchased binding. Bias binding may be purchased in packages and in many colors. The advantage to self-made binding is that you can use fabrics from your quilt to coordinate colors. Double-fold, straight-grain binding and double-fold, bias-grain binding are two of the most commonly used types of binding.

Double-fold, straight-grain binding is used on smaller projects with right-angle corners. Double-fold, bias-grain binding is best suited for bed-size quilts or quilts with rounded corners.

To make double-fold, straight-grain binding, cut 2"-wide strips of fabric across the width or down the length of the fabric totaling the perimeter of the quilt plus 10". The strips are joined as shown in Figure 17 and pressed in half wrong sides together along the length using an iron on a cotton setting with *no* steam.

Figure 17
Join binding strips in a
diagonal seam to eliminate
bulk as shown.

Lining up the raw edges, place the binding on the top of the quilt and begin sewing (again using the walking foot) approximately 6" from the beginning of the binding strip. Stop sewing 1/4" from the first corner, leave the needle in the quilt, turn and sew diagonally to the corner as shown in Figure 18.

Fold the binding at a 45-degree angle up and away from the quilt as shown in Figure 19 and back down flush with the raw edges. Starting at the top raw edge of the quilt, begin sewing the next side as shown in Figure 20. Repeat at the next three corners.

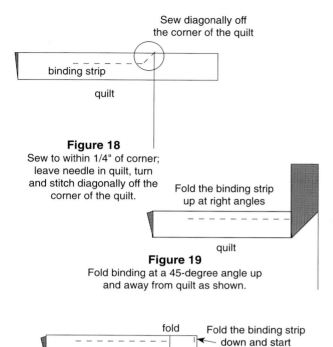

Figure 18
Sew to within 1/4" of corner; leave needle in quilt, turn and stitch diagonally off the corner of the quilt.

Figure 19
Fold binding at a 45-degree angle up and away from quilt as shown.

Figure 20
Fold the binding strips back down, flush with the raw edge, and begin sewing.

As you approach the beginning of the binding strip, stop stitching and overlap the binding 1/2" from the edge; trim. Join the two ends with a 1/4" seam allowance and press the seam open. Reposition the joined binding along the edge of the quilt and resume stitching to the beginning.

To finish, bring the folded edge of the binding over the raw edges and blind-stitch the binding in place over the machine-stitching line on the backside. Hand-miter the corners on the back as shown in Figure 21.

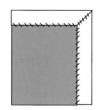

Figure 21
Miter and stitch the corners as shown.

If you are making a quilt to be used on a bed, you will want to use double-fold, bias-grain bindings because the many threads that cross each other along the fold at the edge of the quilt make it a more durable binding.

Cut 2"-wide bias strips from a large square of fabric. Join the strips as illustrated in Figure 17 and press the seams open. Fold the beginning end of the bias strip 1/4" from the raw edge and press. Fold the joined strips in half along the long side, wrong sides together, and press with *no* steam (Figure 22).

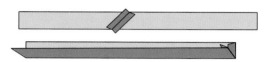

Figure 22
Fold end in and press strip in half.

Follow the same procedures as previously described for preparing the quilt top and sewing the binding to the quilt top. Treat the corners just as you treated them with straight-grain binding. Since you are using bias-grain binding, you do have the option to just eliminate the corners if this option doesn't interfere with the patchwork in the quilt. Round the corners off by placing one of your dinner plates at the corner and rotary-cutting the gentle curve (Figure 23).

Figure 23
Round corners to eliminate square-corner finishes.

As you approach the beginning of the binding strip, stop stitching and lay the end across the beginning so it will slip inside the fold. Cut the end at a 45-degree angle so the raw edges are contained inside the beginning of the strip (Figure 24). Resume stitching to the beginning. Bring the fold to the back of the quilt and hand-stitch as previously described.

Figure 24
End the binding strips as shown.

Overlapped corners are not quite as easy as rounded ones, but a bit easier than mitering. To make overlapped corners, sew binding strips to opposite sides of the quilt top. Stitch edges down to finish. Trim ends even.

Sew a strip to each remaining side, leaving 1 1/2"–2" excess at each end. Turn quilt over and fold binding down even with previous finished edge as shown in Figure 25.

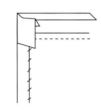

Figure 25
Fold end of binding even with
previous edge.

Fold binding in toward quilt and stitch down as before, enclosing the previous bound edge in the seam. It may be necessary to trim the folded-down section to reduce bulk as shown in Figure 26.

Figure 26
An overlapped corner is not quite as
neat as a mitered corner.

FINAL TOUCHES

If your quilt will be hung on the wall, a hanging sleeve is required. Other options include purchased plastic rings or fabric tabs. The best choice is a fabric sleeve, which will evenly distribute the weight of the quilt across the top edge, rather than at selected spots where tabs or rings are stitched,

and keep the quilt hanging straight and not damage the batting.

To make a sleeve, measure across the top of the finished quilt. Cut an 8"-wide piece of muslin equal to that length—you may need to seam several muslin strips together to make the required length.

Fold in 1/4" on each end of the muslin strip and press. Fold again and stitch to hold. Fold the muslin strip lengthwise with right sides together. Sew along the long side to make a tube. Turn the tube right side out; press with seam at bottom or centered on the back.

Hand-stitch the tube along the top of the quilt and the bottom of the tube to the quilt back making sure the quilt lies flat. Stitches should not go through to the front of the quilt and don't need to be too close together as shown in Figure 27.

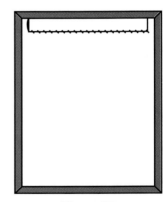

Figure 27
Sew a sleeve to the top back of the quilt.

Slip a wooden dowel or long curtain rod through the sleeve to hang.

When the quilt is finally complete, it should be signed and dated. Use a permanent pen on the back of the quilt. Other methods include cross-stitching your name and date on the front or back or making a permanent label which may be stitched to the back.

Special Thanks

We would like to thank the talented quilt designers whose work is featured in this collection.

Connie Ark
Quilted Holiday Cards, 29

Ann Boyce
Hannukkah Star Quilt, 41
Dog Days of Summer, 92
Stars & Stripes, 99
Happy Birthday Wall Quilt, 123

Michele Crawford
Columbus Sets Sail, 141

Holly Daniels
Stained-Glass Cross, 63

Diana DiPaolo
Lucky Shamrock, 59
Bunnies in a Basket, 65

Lucy A. Fazely
Sunflower Sensation, 137
Cobweb, 147
Pumpkin Delivery, 155

Sue Harvey
A Tree for All Seasons, 79

Wendy Kinzler
Family Tree Anniversary Quilt, 145

Janice McKee
Mother's Day Basket, 69

Anita Murphy
Home for Christmas Banner, 33

Connie Rand
Flowers at the Office, 48
Thanksgiving, 159

Jill Reber
Sweetheart Roses, 43
Born on the Fourth of July, 103
My Grandpa's Bow Ties, 127

Christine Schultz
Holly Berry Santa Wall Quilt, 35
Home in the Garden, 95
Bear Paw Quilt, 132

Marian Shenk
Bear Babies, 73

Charlyne Stewart
Confetti Wall Quilt, 15
Summer Sailing, 115
Summer Vest, 119

Norma Storm
Hedgehog in the Morning, 21
Piggy Parade, 53
Welcome Wreath, 87
Fireworks, 105

Joy Tennell
Snowman Cardigan, 17
Gingerbread Men Sweatshirt, 25
Poinsettia Vest, 27

Jodi G. Warner
Snowstars Wall Quilt, 8
Autumn Wreath, 149

PHOTO CREDITS
Models from Charmaine Model Agency, Fort Wayne, Ind.
Elizabeth Frauhiger, 24 and 130
Chelsea Doyle, 90
Alexis Bradford, 90